Le Guide Officiel To Becoming British

How to Fit In If You're French

By Muriel Demarcus

Copyright © Muriel Demarcus 2016

ISBN-13: 9781533656605

Cover design and typesetting by Vanessa Mendozzi

Back cover photo by Nadia King

Images on cover purchased under license "Shutterstock.com"

Edited by Juliet Gwyn Palmer

All rights reserved

Massive thanks to all my supporters and readers, and especially to my loyal agent, Robert Gwyn Palmer.

'The best thing I know between France and England is the sea.'
Douglas William Jerrold (1803-57) – British writer

Contents

Introduction: Are you ready to become British?   1

EVERYDAY LIFE

How to Speak Proper English	9
Eating and Drinking	17
How to Dress	25
Transport	33

RELATIONSHIPS

Making Friends	45
Dating	51
The Sex Issue	55

WORKING IN THE UK

Is It Worth It?	69
A British Education	71
How to Find a Job and Get Promoted	79
Setting Up a Business	83

BRITISH CULTURE AND VALUES

Some Things You Should Know	91
Behaving British	97

CUSTOMS, IDIOSYNCRASIES AND THE WIDER WORLD

British Ways   109
The Bigger Picture   121

Conclusion: So what about me?   127

About the author   131

INTRODUCTION
ARE YOU READY TO BECOME BRITISH?

I'll always remember the day my husband came back home saying that he'd had a very tempting job offer in London. I was faced with a difficult choice: I could follow him and change job, or change husband. I know it sounds like an easy choice, but it wasn't. My job in Paris was an important part of my identity: I'd spent long years studying at very selective universities to get it. Added to that, I'd studied German, not English, as a foreign language. It's a French thing: German is supposed to get you into better classes. What I'm trying to say is that I could barely ask for directions in English. It wasn't going to be a walk in the park.

I ended up following my husband, and we all moved to London.

Fast-forward fourteen years or so, and we're still living in Great Britain. We all have British passports. I'm asked all the time why I made the decision to become British. I already have a European passport – I'm French-born. Until the referendum on Brexit, there was no real need to be naturalised. Most – if not all – of my expat friends didn't want to become British. It's a long and expensive process: you need to get your permanent residence card first, then pass a test, then pay a hefty fee, then attend a citizenship ceremony, and finally get interviewed for your first passport. Why would you put yourself through such a hassle? It's difficult to explain. It happened gradually, I suppose. I just turned a corner after four or five years of living in the UK and there was no going back. I didn't see it coming, but I ended up loving it here. I just caught the British bug, and there's no cure for it.

It might have helped that I didn't struggle as much as I'd anticipated when I first arrived because there were French people everywhere. Slowly but surely my English improved, and it wasn't long before I wasn't ashamed any more to speak English with my strong French accent. I haven't stopped talking ever since.

My children started to answer me in English. They were very happy in their respective schools. We had bangers and mash at home. We were becoming a fully-fledged British family.

I also started to resent the negativity of my French friends, who kept complaining about paying the – ridiculously low – French university fees and about the – fantastic – French healthcare. I started to enjoy the British sense of humour. I'm conscious that I still have a lot to learn, as I sometimes get the joke a couple of days late.

I'm nowhere near understanding the causes of my slow drift towards British citizenship. But I know what sort of symptoms you should watch out for to check whether you've caught the same bug as me. Here's a short list of five easy questions. I urge you to take the test immediately, because at least you'll know where you stand.

First Question:
Do you pour the tea before the milk or the milk before the tea?

What do you think?

Answer:
It doesn't matter. What does matter is that your answer must be more than a hundred words long (preferably longer) and that you make your position in the class system abundantly clear by declaring a preference for one way or the other: milk first = working class, milk last = middle class and upwards.

Second Question:
Your new neighbour is putting his rubbish out in front of his house for collection. He's in his boxers (and nothing else despite the biting cold). You have to walk close by him as you're going to the Tube station.

How do you behave?

Answer:
Just pretend it's totally normal to be outside with almost no clothes on. Make small talk, but from a safe distance. Be polite. Think along the following lines:

'Hello! It's getting colder, isn't it?'

'Hi! Lovely to finally put a [small pause] … face to a name!'

Don't blush, don't stay silent. Don't make fun of the situation, it would be rude. Even if it's extremely tempting, don't say, 'I hadn't realised that stripes were making a comeback!' You don't want to take (too much) advantage of the situation just yet. It's a question of timing.

Third Question:
In which section of the supermarket do you find Yorkshire puddings?

Answer:
Not in the biscuits and pudding section. Try the frozen section, silly!

However, the real test of Britishness is whether or not you can make your own Yorkshire puddings. Apparently it's all about the cooking oil being warm enough. For most of us non-natives it would be wise to assume that mastering the art of making Yorkshire pudding is simply unattainable.

Fourth Question:
How much time does a British guy need to make a move on someone he likes?

Answer:
This is a tricky one. The general consensus is that two months is an absolute minimum, and you should expect hours of small talk about useless matters before the guy will give you a hint of his feelings. There are cases when it can be years or even decades. As a general rule, you should also know that most declarations of love happen down the pub after one too many pints and need to be reconfirmed the morning after the night before to avoid any disappointment.

Fifth Question:
You're very late for an important job interview because your child threw up on your outfit and you had to change just before leaving home. There's worse: there's a signal failure on the Tube and you get stuck for half an hour on the Underground.

How do you behave when you finally make it to the interview?

Answer:
Pull yourself together, for God's sake! A stiff upper lip is absolutely de rigueur, even if you're so upset you want to cry. (Someone who has 'a stiff upper lip' does not show their feelings when they're upset.) Play it down and say something like, 'There was a little bit of a blooper this morning …' Make it look like it was one of those things. Apologise, but not too much. It's not your fault. And get the job, of course.

So, be honest now: how did you fare? You know by now that it's hard work becoming British, so if you're drifting that way, you need to know. If you got correct answers for at least two of these questions, here's what I would say to you: watch out! You're getting there without even realizing it!

This guide will give you useful tips and insights to help you integrate as painlessly as possible. Believe me: if it happened to me, it can happen to any of us.

EVERYDAY LIFE

HOW TO SPEAK PROPER ENGLISH

'A man who speaks three languages is trilingual. A man who speaks two languages is bilingual. A man who speaks one language is English.'
Claude Gagnière (1928–2003), French writer

You might think that because you were taught to speak English at school or at work you'll be fine, but you couldn't be more wrong. The British are very precise about how things must be said. Here are a few tricks that will go a long way towards helping you gain a better understanding of what the British really mean and make sure that they understand you.

Use as many words as possible
A simple 'yes' in response to a question will betray the fact that you're not familiar with the way people talk over here. You need to say instead, 'Well, I sort of said I would.' Or, 'Yes, I hear what you say.' Keep the words coming out at any cost.

In the same vein, never say no. Except in a life-or-death situation, maybe. 'No' is much too direct. It closes the debate and the British love to spin things out. Instead, you can always buy time by saying, 'That's an interesting point of view, isn't it?'

OK, let's practise now. Let's suppose that someone tells you: 'Boys and girls need to be educated separately because they learn in different ways.' As you may know, we French feel strongly that this is a backwards idea coming straight from the Middle Ages. Well, you mustn't say so. Bite your tongue. Breathe. Say something like, 'That's an interesting point of view. For my part, I totally enjoyed being educated with boys during my childhood.' Can you spot the difference?

Pay attention to what's *not* said

You need to question everything you're told. 'Is this school any good?' I asked one of my friends. 'Oh yes, it's a good school,' she said. 'Very sporty.' What she meant was that they weren't very good academically. But how could I have guessed? It took long years of practice to get the message. I'm still working on it.

Learn how a sentence can mean one thing whilst also its complete opposite

One day I was reading about what seemed to be a clear-cut corruption case in one of the leading newspapers. But the journalist had concluded that 'There [was] no clear evidence of corruption'.

On the face of it, it's a simple sentence. But, as you'll find out, appearances can be deceptive. What does this sentence even mean? Does it mean that the guy hadn't done anything wrong? Or does it mean that there was unclear evidence of corruption – in which case he actually had done something wrong? The English language had allowed the journalist to keep all options open, and that's exactly what he'd done. Why would he have taken a position? No need to. It's much easier not to make a decision.

The same goes with another expression the British will keep using at every possible opportunity:

'I don't disagree.'

This one still baffles me. Technically, if your acquaintance doesn't disagree then he/she must agree. But then, he/she has chosen not to simply say that he/she agrees. Why? Probably because, deep down, he/she doesn't agree – see, one thing and its opposite again. I've come to the conclusion that the person you're talking to doesn't care about what you're saying, probably disagrees, and is looking for an easy escape. But don't ask for any clarification unless you have a couple of hours to spare.

Don't take English expressions too literally
When I was told by a British colleague that we should touch base the following week, I panicked. When I found out that touching base had nothing to do with touching your base (or anyone else's), I couldn't help being relieved!

The same goes for lots of idioms and expressions, like 'getting your knickers in a twist', and 'belt and braces'; and when the actress talks to the bishop, there might be no actress and no bishop. Now you're warned. (You're welcome.)

Likewise, when you're being called 'darling', 'sweetheart', 'honey' or even 'pumpkin', don't worry. They don't mean it. Most of the time. One day, a cab driver, right after calling me 'love', asked me whether I wanted him to keep me company that night. I politely declined, thinking that it was another British thing. With hindsight, I'm not so sure. I suppose we all have to learn, and I'm no exception.

Know how to make sense when you're talking nonsense
Don't underestimate such a vital skill. If you want to blend in, you'll have to learn.

When I moved to this country, these are the sorts of things I would have said:

- Where are the children? It's very quiet in here;
- I don't speak English very well;
- The proposal was rejected;
- She's divorced but doesn't want anyone to know;
- I went to the concert on my own;
- I disagree;
- I don't understand.

Fatal mistakes. Everybody noticed that I hadn't been brought up in Britain, despite the fact that my English was, I know, grammatically correct. Here's what I should have said:

- Where are the kids? I thought it seemed a bit quiet!
- I'm an 'advanced beginner' in English;
- The proposal was rejected as a whole, but there were some good points;
- Her divorce is an open secret;
- I went on my own to a very popular concert;
- Let's agree to disagree;
- It's a bit opaque.

As you might guess, it was, and still is, a steep learning curve. I'm not sure that I'll ever get there. This is because my brain is wired in a different way. I have to learn to think and speak in a new way. It's hard work. It's all about giving a good account of yourself and making the right impression, whereas I was brought up to be straightforward and direct. (And discreet). No wonder I'm struggling. When does it get better?

Understand what the British mean

The meaning of some words can be deceptive over here. Before I draw any conclusions as to what somebody really means, I have to take a step back and analyse how things were said, when and why. And, despite my best efforts, sometimes I still don't get it. I'm ashamed to admit it: I've given up more than once. Sad but true.

Let me give you an example. A friend of mine had just had a baby and she was a bit overweight. She wasn't bothered by it at all, and even told me, 'People are so nice! They all say I look so well.'

That was when it dawned on me. Over here, when you're told that you look 'well', it means, more often than not, that you're fat, or you've put on weight. Alternatively, your British friends might be implying that you've lost weight but don't want to infer that you were fat before (and still are a little bit). I too was told after my pregnancies, 'Oh! You look well!' I did indeed look well. All too 'well', to be honest. It all makes sense now. How come I hadn't noticed before? Why hadn't anyone told me?

If you look *really* well (as in, not fat), then people will tell you that you look 'great' or even 'amazing'. Or they won't say anything at all because they might be a bit jealous.

I've now established that 'well' means 'fat' *most* of the time. However, it's all a question of circumstances. For instance, if you don't know what to say to someone you haven't seen for a long time, it can be normal to say, 'Hi! You look well,' and not mean much – it's just supposed to be polite. Life is complicated this side of the Channel.

Likewise, when something is 'interesting', it usually means that it's complete crap. Now you've been warned. And if you're told that you 'almost' did something, it means that you're not there yet, at all.

Don't worry, I told you it's a steep learning curve. It will take years of effort to become a master of the English language. On the plus side, it can be fun – once you get the hang of all the subtle nuances of the British language, that is.

BAROMETER

Question:
You've just been on a date with someone who didn't look at all like her/his online profile picture. Your friend asks you what happened. What do you say?

Answers:
1. 'He/she looked like the back of a bus.'
2. 'His/her picture was very nicely taken.' (You're already British, aren't you?)
3. 'He/she was such a lovely boy/girl.' (You're getting there).

Question:
You're reading a very boring book. Someone asks you what your opinion of the book is. What do you reply?

Answers:
1. 'It's an interesting concept. I've never read anything like it before.' (Very British indeed.)
2. 'I'm not sure I'll manage to finish it.' (Are you sure you're not French?)
3. You don't answer anything. (Are you sure you're an adult? You might be missing an opportunity to make a new friend, which doesn't happen that often in the UK.)

EATING AND DRINKING

'English cooking: if it's cold, it's soup. If it's warm, it's beer.'
Anonymous French person

Complaining about the food in the UK is the favourite pastime of most expats. From bad sandwiches at lunch to junk food, the UK's reputation for bad food is such that even today my family sends me a parcel of French food every month or so. I've tried to explain many times that we're fine and have everything we need, but they don't believe me. Mind you, it's all about knowing where to shop. Just like in every city around the world.

French food is probably what I miss most in London. When I lived in Paris, I bought fresh bread every day at the local *boulangerie*. It wasn't a luxury – most people did it. And there was at least one *boulangerie* every hundred metres. Furthermore, after a day of work I used to stop at my local butcher or fishmonger to buy something fresh for dinner. What I was cooking wasn't complicated, but it was healthy and tasty – usually something grilled, with vegetables and a touch of olive oil.

Initially, in London, I felt lost. The bread came so tightly wrapped in plastic that it also tasted like plastic. I realised that I was, without knowing it, addicted to good, simple, artisan food. When I looked at my colleagues biting into their sandwiches – made of soft and soulless processed bread – I hurt inside. Worst of all, I used to offer my friends coming round, as a treat, fresh baguettes found in exclusive gourmet shops after hours of research. Instead of appreciating it, they were so blissfully unaware of what good bread tasted like that they told me my baguette was overbaked. They simply weren't used to fresh bread: the loud crack of the firm crust, followed by the soft noise ('squish') made by the inside. Philistines. They don't know what they don't know. They're not educated in good food. I will not and cannot *ever* get used to eating crappy bread and processed food. Clear and simple.

To be fair, French food can be complicated in its own way – thinking of snails and frogs' legs – but that's not what I'm talking about here. Some days I'd kill to get something simple and fresh (and not *fried*, please) that doesn't come in a tightly wrapped little box. In order to survive in London, I had to develop new skills – such as how to bake my own bread. I'm proud to say I managed. But it's hard work.

In order to speed up your integration, I thought I should give you a couple of examples of British specialities that you can safely try, and explain about the eating and drinking habits over here. Don't expect it to be easy. It will be up to you to know where to find food that you like. And it will be a tough ride if you don't like sandwiches!

Lemon drizzle cake

It's fair to say that lemon drizzle cake is the only kind of drizzle I love. Why do I like it so much? The secret of such a cake is that it's moist. It melts in the mouth. In order to achieve this pure state of perfection, you have first to bake a lemon cake. Once it's ready and slightly cooled, you have to dig little holes in it and fill them with a mixture of lemon juice, sugar and, if you fancy, the lemon zest. You need to do this carefully and make sure that the cake absorbs the juice. It will totally be worth it in the end. You need to eat the cake reasonably fast, otherwise it becomes a bit drier (which is less nice, I must admit). So you have the perfect excuse to stuff your face immediately.

Now, I need to clarify something: in our home country, you're not supposed to dip your bread/toast/cake/biscuit/whatever in your morning tea or coffee (although the British do this in what they imagine to be 'true French fashion', dipping their croissant into their *café-au-lait* in an artisan bowl all the way from Habitat, or maybe IKEA). It's rude. But the beauty of the lemon drizzle cake is that it's pre-dipped for you! What's not to like about it? Don't you agree that this is a perfect example of British pragmatism?

As I am sure you've understood, I highly recommend lemon drizzle cakes to get yourself accustomed to British cake.

In the same vein, sticky toffee pudding can safely be tried, but preferably during winter. There can surely be few things better than a warm, dense slice of oozing sticky toffee pudding on a cold evening. It's so good that it should come with a warning: one bite and you won't be able to stop.

Now, I would recommend avoiding at all costs the following desserts: banoffee pie, carrot cake, spotted dick (a sweet, spongy suet roll with currants in it), jam roly-poly, lardy cake, Sussex pond pudding, Battenberg cake or rainbow cake (unless you like your system to be full of chemical dye) and clootie dumpling. This is because in the best case scenario they all taste worse than they look. Been there, done it, and, honestly, it's not worth it.

The 'fry-up' or British breakfast
I was brought up to have a piece of bread or some cereal for breakfast, with coffee or tea. That was it. It was a nice start to the day, and I got used to it.

Over here, things are completely different. It's perfectly normal to have fried eggs, fried bread, sausages, bacon and baked beans for breakfast. Come to think of it, you can have anything, as long as it's fried. And the more, the better. The plates they use look like dishes to me, and the portions could feed a giant.

The smell of fried oil first thing the morning used to make my stomach churn. When you walk to work in London, you can see all the office workers having huge British breakfasts in coffee shops Where I used to work, it was common practice to turn your computer on and then go to the canteen and come back with a plastic box full of goodies such as fried wedges, fried eggs and the mandatory bacon. I'll let you imagine the smell (and chewing noises) while I was replying to my emails. Initially I found the whole thing completely disgusting. But over time I found out that the fry-up is the best way to get back to business after a hangover. Enough said. Now you know.

You'll need to be very cautious with some food: I recommend taking things very slowly with porridge, chutney and Blue Stilton, for instance. Don't be put off by a vomit-like texture. You'll get used to it. Eventually. (I have to say, I'm still extremely cautious.)

And don't look surprised if you're served a mint sauce or even jam with your Sunday roast over here; it's completely normal. You can always leave it on the side. Well, most of the time, anyway, because sometimes it's already poured on and you have no choice but to eat it with your meat. Not nice …

Finally, I'd like to add that you can safely eat mince pies: they have no meat in them. (Don't laugh, but it took me four whole years to figure this out.) Truly, they taste quite nice.

Tea

If you're invited to have tea, it can mean different things. For instance, 'having tea' can mean having an extra early dinner. You can forget about having dinner at a civilised time like 7.30 p.m. in the UK. Be prepared for having 'tea' at around 6 p.m., sometimes even earlier, because your kids will be starving after all the after-school activities. This means that you'll be hungry again later in the evening, and will need a top-up. No wonder we put on weight so easily over here!

However, 'having tea' can also refer to having a posh cup of tea and various sandwiches (in which case cucumber sandwiches are an absolute must) on social occasions such as attending a cricket match or meeting the Queen. Once again, it's all in the context.

Drinking preferences

This is pretty straightforward. British men drink beer. Beer in England predates other alcoholic drinks produced in London. We French drink wine or champagne. You might prefer other types or alcohol, but if you want to look British, you need to order a lager. Not drinking booze will spark a rumour that you're either pregnant or a recovering alcoholic. British women sometimes drink cheap wine down the pub, which is why I believe it's safer to have a lager as the wine will be disappointing.

And when they're not drinking beer, British men are having a cup of tea. Of course.

Drinking habits

The best way to deal with any sort of problem, personal or professional, is to have a few drinks down the pub.

During summer, you have to try Pimm's with lemonade. It will brighten the dullest of cricket games and you'll be completely off your head for the whole game, which will make it pass much faster. It's also common knowledge that Pimm's lemonade is how mums survive the dreadful Sports Day and Summer Fair.

BAROMETER

Question:
It's cold and damp, and you want to have a heart-warming dessert. What will you have?

Answer:
You can have scones, apple pie, Eccles cakes or even plum pudding (or whatever you like), but you need to have it with ice cream. The love affair of the British with ice cream knows no limits. Even when everybody's shivering outside, the British eat ice cream. It's an essential part of the British diet, and there is simply no avoiding it. If you're serious about becoming British, you'll have to learn to love ice cream even when it's freezing.

Question:
Which is the most calorific?

1. Deep-fried Mars bar
2. Fish and chips
3. Brandy butter
4. Butterscotch sauce

Answer:
It doesn't matter. They're all part of British traditional cuisine and must be treated with love and respect. Just ignore the calorie minefield and go for a run in the snow to burn the calories off after you've stuffed your face.

HOW TO DRESS

> 'When an Englishwoman is dressed, she's no longer a woman, she is a cathedral. You don't seduce her, you demolish her.'
> Paul Gavarni (1804–66), French artist

Another common complaint of expats in the UK is that they don't know where to find decent clothes. If you're looking for the same brands and looks as at home, then you're bound to fail. British fashion is eclectic and never takes you where you want to go, but should you try something quintessentially British on, you might enjoy the journey. Once you know where to look, you can find everything you want in London, and choose either to discover future star designers or to stick to classics. Just go to Brick Lane market if you don't believe me.

The beauty of London lies elsewhere. Over here, you'll never feel (too) judged. I can go to work without any make-up on and nobody bats an eyelid. The other day, the lady behind me was running her errands in her bathrobe. Yep, flip-flops and bathrobe, to be precise. The shop attendant didn't flicker. Apparently, it's completely normal, nothing to worry about. I knew about going outside in your PJs, but I'd never seen anyone in a bathrobe on the street before. I suppose I still have a lot to learn. Just so you know, though, I'm still much too French to go out in my bathrobe. I just couldn't open the front door. It must be something in my genes. Except maybe if the house was on fire.

So, here are some quick tips on going native

Don't be afraid of stripes and colours
Beware: the British are fixated with stripes. They're on the Tube, at work, in the street … I'm not talking about the discreet little stripes on a white shirt here, but of the thick, usually purple or green ones (at the time of writing). My favourite is stripes on a pink shirt. They're usually trying to cover a fat, well-fed tummy, but with limited success. Some men will simply never learn. And some women will always think that it makes them look thinner. Here's a newsflash for you: it doesn't.

What's even better is when, together with the shirt, the trousers have stripes too – not the same ones, hopefully. The possibilities are endless. The jacket might be striped as well, and the tie too –usually oblique ones, to be fair. Some decide to have a tie with dots on to add a little bit of variety. Lovely touch. After careful observation, I've come to the conclusion that stripes give an ego-boost to the guy who wears them. The more stripes, the better, and the smarter he'll feel. They're a sort of trampoline. The more they have, the higher their confidence jumps.

Any colour will do. I've seen a rainbow man. The trousers, the jacket, the tie, everything – with the mandatory stripes, naturally, and everything was a different colour. Pink and orange are also very popular. I'm starting to believe that colour-blindness is much more widespread this side of the Channel.

Nighties

I once went to our local M&S store with a colleague to buy some nighties. The only nighties on display were dotted or with floral prints (and some with both). How can you even consider wearing this, I asked myself? My British colleague explained that it was to keep you warm during the long British winter. She loved a good nightie and bed socks to sleep in.

How can a guy fancy a woman in an M&S nightie? I'm pretty sure it must be the first recommendation of all marriage counsellors: 'Ditch the M&S nighties.'

Unless you want to make it as hard as possible for the poor guy lying next to you. In which case, you need to add some hair rollers and you'll be off sex for at least a year.

My friend asked me what I thought about one of them. I blurted out, 'I wouldn't be seen dead in it!' There you have it. I will only wear nighties if I want to get a divorce. Ditch the nighties. Do it for me.

Wellies

Over here, wellies are not just plastic boots. They're a way of life, and a sign that you love walking in the mud, preferably around your lovely country house. Wellies show that you live a healthy lifestyle, have remained approachable and that, at heart, you're still a country man/woman. The Queen is someone who loves her wellies, and Kate Middleton is photographed with hers at least once a month. (You'll soon notice that there's clearly a wellies war between the royals.) The fact that you might live in London is completely irrelevant. Wellies are a must-have accessory.

For a quintessentially British look, wellies must be worn with short trousers or even with a miniskirt.

Hot pants

We once had to prepare for a dinner and I wanted my teenage daughter to be dressed a little bit more formally than usual. Me being me, I was intending to wear my black dress. You can't go wrong with a little black dress, can you? I couldn't live without my black dress, because it's classic, timeless, flatters the figure, and the length is perfect. As for my daughter, it was a no-brainer: she said she was going to wear her formal hot pants. I was stunned.

Naively, I thought that hot pants could only be something informal, but no, I was wrong – there are hot pants for all sorts of occasions. In British fashion, that is. I have never seen a French woman wear hot pants in a formal setting. You can wear them on the beach during a sunny day, but that's as far as you would go. And given the fact that I don't have the legs of a young girl, I'm not sure I would risk it. Would you? This is yet another fashion schism: hot pants are BIG this side of the Channel, but not in France.

Tweed

Tweed has long been a cloth associated with quintessential Britishness. Tweed instantly makes you look like the lord (or the lady) of the manor. Don't be scared of wearing a tweed blazer with tweed trousers or skirt. Tweed has this amazing capacity to make you look sixty and wealthy, whatever your age and background. Tweed freezes you in time. Tweed is the Botox that removes the wrinkles of British style.

Nudity

The British attitude to nudity is a classic example of double standards. I used to love wearing a short (mid-thigh) skirt in Paris and nobody had any problem with it. I once wore it in London and I could sense that something was odd. People were looking at me in a weird way. Finally, one of the secretaries at the office told me that I was dressed like a fifteen-year-old. Lesson learned. I wear my skirts just above the knee now.

The funny thing is that one of my neighbours (a guy in his sixties, I would say) loves to daydream in his birthday suit in front of his picture window in full view of the whole street – and my house. He also likes to indulge in a little bit of scratching. As tactfully as possible, I tried to explain to him that he should close the curtains. We live in the middle of London; it's not as if he were on his own in the countryside. I was expecting an apology. Cardinal mistake.

All I got was that he would do as he pleased in his house. His wife even asked me whether my children had never seen their father naked, as if that were the issue. She made me sound like a prude.

You'll note that I've never seen *her* naked, just him. Over here, the old boys' network is still alive and kicking, and they believe they can do pretty much everything with complete impunity. And in pure British style, they also threatened to sue me (I'm still figuring out what for. Indecent comment maybe?) On the bright side, he stopped, and I'm pleased to report that I haven't seen him naked for a couple of years now.

I talked to various friends about this, and quickly found out that the naked neighbour issue was a pretty common occurrence. My friend's eighty-year-old neighbour loves to sleep naked in his garden in full view of the adjoining houses. And when he isn't naked, he loves to wear the shortest and smallest possible pants. His wife is always fully clothed.

My mistake was to have dared to make a comment. The British thing to do would have been to pretend that I hadn't seen anything (despite the fact that it was extremely difficult to ignore). I can't believe how French I still am. Some things will never change.

BAROMETER

Question:
You're sitting with a friend in a Motcomb Street coffee shop. This is in a very exclusive part of London, Belgravia. You're watching people passing by. You quickly notice that most women have a similar hairstyle. It's a bit weird: they have big hair that's staying perfectly in place despite the wind. Impressive. How is this possible?

Answers:
1. This is not a haircut, this is hair sculpture. It's very fashionable in some parts of London and is unofficially called the soufflé, because you do have a soufflé on your head. (You're fully British.)
2. It's a very exclusive communication network: the ladies use it to call to each other, like birds of the same species across marshland. (You've spent too much time in the countryside.)
3. It's awful. Hideous. And on top of that, it must be ridiculously expensive. (No, no, no: even if it's true, that's simply not what you say in London.)

Question:
From time to time – I would say at least once a month – some well-meaning friends or acquaintances will tell you that you look very French/Italian/Polish/German (whatever your nationality is). What do they mean?

Answers:

1. They're just saying it for the sake of it. (You're probably right. You need to get used to it, because it'll happen a lot.) In my case, I thought it was the way I dressed. But as I'm very low-maintenance, that was highly unlikely. The thing is, I'm not skinny (and, for the record, I'm not fat: I'm somewhere in between, like most of us), and I don't smoke like a chimney. The thing is, I don't smoke at all. And, as I've been told many times, French women smoke. So why do I look French again? I'll never get it.
2. They mean you don't belong here. (You're far too sensitive, dear: it's meant in the nicest possible way.) You can always reply 'You look very British' if you want to make a point.
3. They mean you bought your clothes in a different country. (Be careful. It might be a compliment. But you never know.)

TRANSPORT

*'I never saw an ugly thing in my life ... Light,
shade and perspective will always make it beautiful.'*
John Constable (1779–1837), British painter

Obviously John Constable hadn't been on the London Tube ...

How do you get around in London? You are, in theory, spoilt for choice: TfL buses, the Tube, the Overground and the tramways are always an Oyster card's touch away ... The sad reality is that, during peak hours, and despite the fact that Tube tickets in London are probably the most expensive in the whole world, it will be extremely busy. Most Londoners walk everywhere they can. It's their secret for keeping fit. Others cycle everywhere, some on the famous 'Boris bikes', and have learned the difficult art of holding an umbrella while cycling. I'm told that an extremely talented elite can even text at the same time. Impressive.

Tubes and trains

In London, unless you can afford a driver (and let's face it, most of us can't), you have to take the Tube. Taking the Tube is, in itself, quite an experience. You can see London Underground staff in their blue and grey uniforms everywhere: at the gates, on the platform, and if you're lucky they might even have a hat on. The whole thing exhibits an outdated charm. What never ceases to amaze me is the small size of the tunnels, with the trains just fitting inside. Woooosh! Most of the trains have been upgraded and brand-new signalling systems have been installed, which is great, but it's taking a long time to fine-tune, hence the numerous closures Londoners have to put up with almost every weekend. To cut a long story short, the trains still have drivers but the driving is completely automatic: the driver is there in case of an emergency, to open and close the doors, and to communicate with the passengers in case of 'incidents', which still happen a lot. As a result of the upgrade, trains are much faster and more frequent. This also means that they gain speed and brake much more abruptly, and the ride is generally less smooth than manually-driven trains.

I take the Victoria line quite a lot, and I like to sit at the end of the carriage, right next to the door. It looks more like a bench, and you half stand (or half sit, depending on how you think of it). We were once arriving at Victoria station when the train started to brake quite violently – due to the automatic driving, probably – and the young man standing in front of me – I would say he was in his early twenties – forgot to hold on to the bar and fell into my arms. To be fair, he almost managed to stop falling when he was one inch from me, but then the train gained speed, he lost his balance again, and smoothly landed right on top of me. He apologised profusely while I tried hard not to laugh. Then, just to rub it in, I said, 'The pleasure was all mine.' He blushed; at this point I was laughing. He then exited the train as fast as he could. The whole thing made my day and I couldn't help smiling for the rest of it. I'm pretty sure the new signalling systems have contributed to many new encounters. I think London Underground should start charging for every relationship they start. This would help their funding issues immensely.

Driving in London

Driving in London is easier than driving in Paris. People are much less aggressive and generally more polite. Having said that, you need to be prepared to face new challenges over here. Here's what I had to deal with the other day:

For once we were on time for the school run. I was pleased with myself. I was about to make a left turn when I saw them: horses. At least fifty of them. The traffic had come to a standstill. Damn it.

That's one of the beauties of living in London. You can get stuck on one of the main streets during rush hour because the Royal Horse Guards are taking their horses to Hyde Park for a morning training session. Lucky me.

There was nothing to do but wait. So we waited, and moved very, very slowly. Eventually the horses made a right turn. Phew! My 'Chelsea tractor' was right behind the last one. I was beginning to feel relieved when, as luck would have it, the horse lifted his tail just before turning and mischievously started defecating on my car. The law of gravity can be deceptive: something fell on one of the car's front lights. I can't understand how it happened, but it did. Yuck!

The Guard found it absolutely hilarious. I was a bit, well, surprised, but I suppose you've got to keep learning, even at my age, and this was definitely a situation I'd never encountered before.

Maybe it's part of the exam to get your driving licence over here. How do you react at the wheel when a horse decides to leave a parting present on your car? They should add this to the citizenship test too.

Anyway, we made it to school eventually and nobody said anything about the car.

Driving on the other side of the road

For years I've used my French driving licence to drive around in London. There's nothing wrong with this, but it couldn't last for ever, could it? If I lost my French driving licence, it would be a nightmare to replace it. I therefore decided to take the plunge and get a British one. It felt a bit like my 'Frenchness' was slowly fading away, but hey, what could I do?

In France, you go to the *prefecture* to do such things. You take a ticket, you queue, and you get to speak to someone. Things are completely different over here. You print your application form on the DVLA website, you send a cheque (because nothing comes for free) and you wait. As I had to send my original driving licence, I have to admit that I was a bit worried. What would happen if they lost it?

But ten days later I received my British driving licence. It felt a bit weird. My French friends keep asking me what it feels like to drive on the wrong side. My British friends also ask exactly the same question. This is typical, isn't it? That's why French and British can't understand each other: they drive on each other's wrong side!

I try to explain that there's no right or wrong side, and they look at me as if I'm mad. I say that it's all a question of habit, and you need to be, you know, flexible. But no, they don't hear me. You have to choose your side, they say. French or British. Right or left.

Let's be clear, I find the British much more civilised at the wheel. They help you whenever they can, which is completely unheard of in France: a friend of mine told me that she missed her exit on the *périphérique* because nobody would let her change lane, and she ended up having to go all round Paris a second time. As you'd expect, there's the occasional mad driver in the UK too, usually in a white van and tooting the horn because you dared to stop your car when someone was crossing the road. But it remains the exception. The thing that still baffles me is the fact that most streets, especially in the countryside, are quite narrow, but it remains very fashionable to have a very big 4x4. Go figure.

Parking stories

Parking is so complicated that no one understands it. Even if you have a resident's permit, you can't relax – the rules can be completely different from one street to the next, and I'm still trying to find out whether you can park on a yellow line on Saturdays and Sundays. I'm told that it depends, but I'm not quite sure what on.

A single yellow line is not the same as a double yellow line, and you need to know that red lines are even more of a mystery. Furthermore, despite an otherwise great sense of humour, the British don't joke with parking rules, and after a couple of hours of being parked illegally, your car might be towed and it'll cost you a lot of time and money to get it back.

You will soon realise that you can't escape from parking fines. They use cameras to spot cars parked in the wrong places. You can't hide; nowhere is safe. I suspect they have a special task force dealing with us drivers trying to do the school run. I once got a fine for dropping my daughter off on a double yellow line. We only stayed a couple of seconds, but that was enough for the camera to take a picture of the car. I've been traumatised ever since.

I've given up and pay up for the odd parking ticket from time to time (£60. What a rip-off! In France it's just €15!!!) Some people integrate so well that they become experts at contesting parking fines and do it at every possible opportunity. I'm of the view that you need to choose your battles and this one is simply not worth fighting.

Roundabouts

As you may know, in England there are roundabouts everywhere. They swear by roundabouts over here. Roundabouts are apparently the solution to all traffic problems, without exception. Small junction? No problem, let's put a small roundabout on it. Big junction? Let's put a huge one on it, or even a double or a triple one. There's even a 'magic roundabout' in Swindon: it consists of five mini-roundabouts arranged around a sixth central one. I kid you not. They're thinking of listing it, I'm told. Something to do with reflecting British values such as spontaneous cooperation. (I'm joking. Yes, even we French sometimes do sarcasm. From time to time.)

There's some controversy over whether it was the British (most likely) or the French (which would surprise me very much, but hey, I might be wrong) who invented the concept of the roundabout. The 'roundabout' was apparently invented in England in 1966, and was then deployed all over Europe, Asia and Australia to great effect. For many Americans, it still represents European driving. The 'traffic circle' is much older, dating from the late nineteenth century, and is most commonly found in North America. Some claim it was a French invention. Traffic circles were circular or elliptical islands containing a big central island, usually 300 to 600 feet wide. They were designed for vehicles to enter, merge, circulate, change lanes and exit at relatively high speeds of 30 to 50 mph. Needless to say, people hated traffic circles (the French thing) and loved the roundabouts (the British thing). I'm still unsure as to why, apart maybe from the speed issue – if you drive faster you'll be more prone to serious crashes – and the usual French-bashing.

So why are roundabouts so popular? According to the articles I've read, roundabouts are deemed safer than traditional junctions because their design precludes most high-risk situations. Some experts have explained that there are several reasons why roundabouts help reduce the likelihood and severity of collisions, such as a low travel-speed, no light to beat, and the fact that it's one-way travel.

However, I can't help noticing that more and more roundabouts are being rendered pointless by having traffic lights added to them. So much for all the purists out there.

BAROMETER

Question:
While waiting for the next train, you hear the following announcement: 'Would Inspector Sands please report to the control room immediately?' What do you do?

Answers:
1. Nothing, this message is plainly intended for someone else. (You're so wrong.)
2. You exit the station immediately: this means there's a fire somewhere. (You're probably a Health and Safety executive.)
3. You sigh and stay on the platform: it's common knowledge that the Inspector Sands message means that a fire has been reported. In 90% of cases, it will be a false alarm. You wait patiently and hope that you'll be able to catch your train. (You're probably a London Underground veteran, and you know that most fire alarms are triggered by burnt toast.)

Question:
What's the usual rule for prosecuting speeding cases?

Answers:
1. You need to respect the speed limit: for example, you can get

caught at 32 mph if the speed limit is 30 mph. (Have you been in England for long? I don't think so. NB: since this rule was implemented in France, the number of accidents has dramatically decreased. Who said the French were lax?)
2. You'll be prosecuted if you were above the speed limit by anything over 10% plus 2 mph. So, for instance, they don't tend to prosecute 35 mph in a 30 mph zone. (You are indeed British.)
3. If the worst comes to the worst, you can always spend half a day doing a speed awareness course. It'll cost you a bit of money, but you should be able to keep your points. (That's the option most of us choose. Now you are warned)

Question:
What do you do if the meter is broken and you've parked your car in a Pay & Display space?

Answers:
1. You shrug and don't pay for parking. (Don't be surprised if your car's towed.)
2. You walk until you reach the next meter, even if it's chucking it down. (Very British indeed.)
3. You move your car elsewhere. (Not possible in London because you've been lucky to have found a parking space in the first place.)

RELATIONSHIPS

MAKING FRIENDS

'One in four Englishmen is gay.'
Edith Cresson (b.1934), French prime minister,
angry that men weren't hitting on her on a visit to London

It took me a few years to make British friends. And it took me a few additional years to be invited over to their places and have drinks or dinner with them. I don't mean to say that I was short of friends in London. It's just that most of them, initially, were not British.

Don't get me wrong: from the very start, I had lots of British acquaintances who were friendly and promised to invite me and my family, when all they wanted was for me to manage their French properties or organise their holidays in my home country (for free, of course). I fell into the trap a few times, and then quickly understood that they were not genuinely interested in me. One day, I might set up a business to help them, but I'll charge. Come to think of it, I'll probably make a fortune.

But fear not: over time, you will make some British friends, and even some very good ones, once you know what to talk about and how to behave. It will take time, but it will be worth it in the end.

How to make conversation

Here, when you don't know what to talk about, you just talk about the weather. You simply can't go wrong if you stick to this rule. If there's an awkward silence, all you have to do is to say something along the lines of 'terrible weather, isn't it?' and you can be sure that the conversation will pick up from there.

Talking about the weather can happen anywhere, even in the most unexpected of places. At work, I went to the loo the other day and the lady who was washing her hands next to me started a passionate conversation about how cold the weather had been over last Christmas. I ended up having to pretend that I had an urgent meeting, otherwise we would probably have spent the whole day chatting away.

I'm told that it can happen at any time of the day as well. A friend of mine discussed the weather with her boyfriend as she arrived (very) late home – she was having an affair. Maybe it prevented a row. Or she used it as an excuse to defuse the situation. It worked. Apparently they're still together and probably still discussing the weather from time to time. He doesn't seem to mind.

But why are the Brits obsessed by the weather? London's weather is broadly similar to the weather in Paris. Both cities have a similar number of rainy days every year. To be precise, Paris has twenty-five and London twenty-nine, according to my research. Not that big a difference.

My theory is that the weather represents a danger or a blessing from above, the idea being that such fortunes or misfortunes fall from celestial heights. There's a joke in France that our ancestors, the Gauls, were scared of only one thing: that the sky might fall on their heads. Maybe this obsession with the weather stems from the same fear.

In any event, London is simply gorgeous when the sun is out. The white stucco-fronted houses glow and it sometimes feels like nothing has changed for the last 150 years. I find it reassuring, peaceful even. There's nothing like a ray of sunshine in London.

Paying a compliment

Simply put: don't. Paying a compliment is considered to be rude over here, unless it's immediately followed by something demeaning. Here's an example:

'You look great today: what a change compared to your last outfit!'

It is a universal truth that British men are much too afraid to pay women a compliment anyway. Essentially, they're absolutely terrified of being "open". They never say it as it is. As a result, women in this country have had to develop a sixth sense about what British men mean.

Here are a few examples:

- If he says, 'You've got lovely eyes,' he's either drunk or wants to assault you.
- If he says, 'I'd like to talk about my feelings,' he's totally in love with you.
- If he says, 'You're so demure,' he wants to have sex.
- If he says, 'She's a lovely girl,' he can't stand her.
- If he says, 'She's very bright,' she looks like the back of a bus.

I told you it was wasn't straightforward. You can't say you weren't warned.

Rejection British-style

Brits are very polite. At all times and in all circumstances. They'll always try to make it easier for you by sugar-coating their rebuttals instead of simply saying 'No' or 'You're not wanted'. I once asked a colleague whether he had already used a new software I'd heard about. I thought it was a yes or no type of question. How naive of me. He replied, 'Not directly.' I'm still wondering what he meant. I've come to the conclusion that, in this instance, he just couldn't say no. It must have hurt him. Saying 'No' is a no-no. A true Brit can't say 'no'. They have to window-dress it. The best examples are as follows:

- 'Well, I'm not sure.'
- 'Yes, I hear what you say.' (However nice it is to hear a yes, don't kid yourself. This is a no.)
- 'I don't suppose so.' (This is quite direct – it must be a good friend of yours.)
- 'I'll contemplate it.' (This one is the worst. Once you've

understood that *contemplating* doesn't mean *doing*, you've made a big, big step forward.)

Likewise, when you apply for a job, a school or anything else, you get, most of the time, a very polite rejection letter that reads something like this:

> 'Dear Xxxx,
> Thank you for your application. Unfortunately, we have received a lot of applications of exceptional quality and, despite your breadth of experience, we feel that other candidates might be better suited … '

From time to time, you don't get anything. Radio silence.

I truly believe that the British are just trying to be nice. They're genuinely trying to soften the shock of the rejection. Does it make it easier to be rejected politely?

No, it doesn't. I think I'd prefer an honest explanation as to why I didn't get what I wanted, with quantified justification. (It must be a French thing: I love numbers.) Like:

- What my daughter's grades at her assessment are, and what she would have needed to pass the test.
- Why exactly my CV didn't make the cut.
- How much the other tenant earns and why he got the flat.

Instead, all I get are wishy-washy explanations like:

- 'The personality of your daughter should have shone through during the interview.' (Darling, she's three!)
- 'We feel you're overqualified for the job.'
- 'The flat isn't available any more.'
- 'You're too good for me.' (Used by my friend's boyfriend to dump her. A classic, apparently.)

Why are they so polite? Why do I hate it? Why is it so difficult to say 'No'? I don't understand. I just don't get it. Please just say no, because rejection should be like taking off a Band-Aid: to the point and quick.

Even if you don't agree with such an approach, you'll need to learn to be polite too, because Brits are so sensitive that if someone tells them what they truly think of them, they have to go and have a little weep in the corner. They need the sugar-coating. Are they wimps? I sometimes wonder.

DATING

> *'It's a shame that British boyfriends don't come with a set of instructions.'*
> J., former trainee

Be patient

How pushy, exactly, is too pushy? Who takes the initiative? To make things difficult, what's considered good practice in London might be unacceptable elsewhere. Life can be difficult. It feels a bit like driving in the dark with only your sidelights on.

A lovely French trainee came to work with us in London. She was funny, cute and very bright. She was also very French and chain-smoked. All the male colleagues in the office used to rush outside whenever she was having a cigarette. She started liking this English guy and, eventually, he took her on a date. She was palpably excited about the whole thing. Except that the following morning she explained to me that he'd behaved like a perfect gentleman and hadn't even tried to kiss her. He'd driven her home and even waited for her to open her entrance door to make sure she was safe, but nothing else had happened. How odd.

She was confused. So was I. As I've never dated a British guy, I couldn't offer any advice. So we did our research (how did we manage before Google?) and asked around. Apparently, some guys wait a bit before making a move. 'OK', she said. 'I can wait.'

And wait she did. Five more dates down the road, and still he hadn't made a move. This couldn't happen in France. She didn't know what to do. I suggested dating continental guys, because I used to find it a lot easier to know where I stood with them – better the devil you know and all that – but she wanted to persevere. We had a quick brainstorm. At the time, I was trying to get my daughter into a local Catholic school and found out that I needed a priest's reference. I was asked for another priest's reference to join a private library around the corner, which I found odd. So I told her that maybe in this country you need a priest's reference before starting a relationship? We asked around but no, apparently it wasn't necessary.

We tried to find other explanations. If he didn't fancy her, why would he keep inviting her to nice restaurants? The trainee, who was not a quitter, decided that he was simply too shy to make a move (maybe it was because of his boarding-school education?), and one evening, after two months of lovely but unsuccessful dates, she invited him to the pub. After a few drinks, she took him to a dark corner of a beautiful mews and tried to kiss him. Fatal mistake. He didn't respond well to her initiative (that's a euphemism) and she felt very ashamed. So ashamed that she cut her work placement short a couple of weeks later, after profusely apologising to the guy. (She argued that she was drunk; he seemed to buy it.)

I bumped into my former English colleague a few months later. He was still single and living with his dog.

This is an extreme story, and I've heard about cases where the British guy eventually managed to share his feelings just before his date was going to close the car door on him when he'd driven her back to her place. But sometimes it's simply too difficult for British guys to make a move.

Online dating

It's an open secret that online dating is huge in the UK. You're not supposed to say that you've met your date online, but it happens all the time. Everybody does it. How you present yourself in your profile is absolutely critical, and you need to follow three cardinal rules.

Rule 1: Do not pose with your pet – otherwise it seems like you're already in a relationship with it. Yes, even if you're a cat person.

Rule 2: Even if you love words, try to keep it short. This is not a therapy session, for God's sake. Even if you have issues that need to be addressed, this is not the place to explain them to the whole world.

Rule 3: Everybody lies about age, weight, and so on. Get over it. You need to see it as a way of enhancing the truth. Nothing personal, and very British indeed: over here, you'll always be told what you want to hear. It's part of the game. Just do what you have to do.

THE SEX ISSUE

'European men and women have sex lives, English men and women have hot water bottles.'
George Mikes (1912–1987), *How to Be an Alien*

Do the British ever have sex?
I can testify that, during the first years we lived in London, nobody ever mentioned the word sex. I was starting to wonder whether it was even part of the vocabulary over here.

Things changed when I moved job and decided to fill in some long overdue questionnaires that a company I had worked for had sent me. (I was doing the occasional freelance job for them. It paid the bills.) I almost fell off my chair.

In the UK, your ethnicity or sexual orientation don't matter except for statistical purposes. In France, such things are considered to be private. You *never, ever* mention them, let alone fill in a questionnaire with your name on it for your company, for whatever purpose it might be. Even more discomfiting, it wasn't the first time I'd worked for this company. Hadn't I already filled this in? I couldn't remember. Why do it a second time? Maybe they thought things had … moved on for me. I couldn't tell.

Right, let's start.

I struggled with the questions on my ethnicity. I could choose *White/Mixed/Asian/Black/Chinese* or *Not stated/please* specify.
So what was I? I could say *White*, but I have some Arab blood. Does that make me mixed, I wondered? The options for mixed were *White and Black Caribbean, White and Black African, White and Asian or Other/please state. I could say Other/White and Arab.* I wasn't too sure about this. If I were to choose *White*, the options were *White British, White Irish* or *Other/please specify*. Should I say *White British*, as I have a British passport? Or should I say *Other/French*? As my grandfather is Italian, should I say *White/French/Italian*. How about *White/French/Italian/British* with a bit of Arab background. Or maybe simply *White/European*.

This was becoming too complicated. I decided to pass.

On to the sexual orientation questionnaire. This was going from bad to worse. Why did they care?

Let's look at the choices:

For our company statistics, please state whether you are:

A. heterosexual male
B. heterosexual female
C. homosexual male
D. homosexual female
E. bisexual male
F. bisexual female
G. male to female transgender
H. female to male transgender
I. other (please specify)

I started wondering what the last category was. This was all becoming too much for me, and I was still deep in thought when a friend of mine joined me for lunch. I decided to have a glass of wine with her. (I don't normally drink during the day, but all these boxes I had to tick were freaking me out.) I must admit that filling in the questionnaires with a couple of glasses of wine in my system was a lot easier. I can't remember what I decided to put in the end, but soon enough I hit the 'send' button. I was pleased to be over and done with the whole thing.

But I'd spoken too soon. Of course I had. An hour later, the HR assistant called me to let me know that I'd forgotten the questionnaire about my religious background. No, is there another questionnaire? Where does it stop? What do they want to know now?

Do they also need to know my knicker size?

On the bright side, because of the questionnaire, I started asking what the last category was about, and it gave me the opportunity to discuss sex with my British friends. We haven't stopped since.

Oh, and 'other' can be hermaphrodite, asexual, pre-op transsexual, pansexual, queer, etc.

Oversharing

We've all had to deal with oversharers. An urge to relate all the graphic details of their latest stomach bug, for instance. This can be quite helpful if it's done over lunch, as you're sure not to be hungry for a while.

Others will give you all the details of their latest surgical operation. You'll have a full explanation of their treatment, how the procedure went, how long it took them to recover, their state of mind, who visited at the hospital, and they will not forget anything. I wouldn't share such details with my close family; I don't know what they're trying to achieve by sharing everything with everyone. I've even seen acquaintances send long weekly emails detailing what's happened to them in gruesome detail. Lovely. Sometimes being kept in the loop is not that great after all.

Being French induces a different type of oversharing over here. For some reason, now that I've lived in London for some time people love to share their sex and relationship issues with me, especially after a pint or two. I'm starting to wonder whether I should charge to listen to them. I remember having a conversation down the pub with some colleagues, and one of them, out of the blue, told me she was having an affair with a married man. She was asking for my advice. I didn't know what to say. I muttered that, as long as it wasn't with my husband, I didn't care. I certainly didn't want to talk about it. She praised my non-judgemental attitude and I felt like running a mile. She then proceeded to tell me how she'd met him, where they were meeting, what they were doing and even where. She couldn't be stopped and I was extremely embarrassed.

A few weeks later, in similar circumstances, a male colleague of mine who'd just had a baby complained that he didn't have any time to read with his wife in the evening, 'let alone do anything else'. I almost choked on my nibbles, muttered 'Give it some time', and made my excuses to leave. What was going on? Surely he needed to talk to his wife if he wanted to have more sex? It seems that, when drunk, British men often complain that they don't have enough sex. It must be some sort of national sport. Someone needs to explain to them that they're not going to solve the problem that way.

Why do people feel the urge to share such things with me? I wouldn't tell my best friend.

So here it is: I'm not a relationship expert and I don't want to become one. Despite being French, I'm quite shy. I like being discreet. Please don't tell me everything! Because we French tend to keep our private lives, well, private.

How to be cool

It must be said that things have drastically changed in London over the last few years. The British now find it cool to shout about their sex life from the rooftops. Worse than that, the latest trend is to have a 'fluid sexuality', and lots of new words have become extremely popular in a very short period of time. If, like me, you're a heterosexual woman who's been married for the best part of twenty years, you're an old fart. So boring.

Everyone's experimenting, nowadays, with words nobody had heard about a couple of years ago, like androgynous, androsexual, aromantic, asexual, bigender, cisgender, demisexual, gender fluid, pansexual, polyamorous, hesbian, gesbian … and this list is far from being exhaustive.

Nowadays, if you've read *Fifty Shades of Grey* you need to bring it along with you at all times and casually leave it next to you in full view of the whole world, whatever your age or marital status. Because it's cool. It proves that you're still on top of your game, and very open-minded. Handcuffs and whips have gone mainstream for a reason.

On the bus recently, I overheard a teenage girl explaining that she wasn't 'gay' but didn't feel completely straight. She looked barely fourteen, and the whole episode made me feel incredibly uncomfortable.

As much as I believe that everybody has the right to enjoy his/her/their sexuality, I sincerely hope that all this openness is just a craze and that everybody will soon learn to keep their private life private.

Having an affair

I keep reading articles about 'the French' and how extramarital affairs are not that big a deal on the continent. It's not making my life any easier.

Some British men still blush when I talk to them because of my accent. I don't know what they're thinking. Maybe that I'm hitting on them? That I ooze sensuality? That I fancy them? Next time, I'll pretend I'm German. Or Swiss. Most middle-aged British men are not listening to what I say for the first five minutes (sometimes even longer). Then, usually, I get a comment like 'You look very French'. I retaliate 'You sound very British'. Or I just smile. Most of the time, I give up and try to work with women. Much easier.

I used to find the whole thing flattering. Now I'm just tired of it. Give me a break. Being French and a woman is a double whammy: you've got to fight against the sexist clichés and the stereotypes against the French. You need a good dose of patience and it's important to keep things in perspective: it's a cultural thing, nothing personal. I've learned to ignore the winks and the smiles after an allusion to the behaviour of Dominique Strauss-Kahn, Francois Hollande and the like.

Over here, they make it sound like the French invented extramarital affairs. Articles usually paint an idyllic picture of open marriages and glorify women who swallow their pride while their husbands follow their roving eye. Apparently, being unfaithful is not that big a deal in France.

What a load of rubbish!

Come on, affairs are not the privilege of the French. Over here, there are plenty of websites for married people who want to cheat on their partner. Such sites might exist in France, but apparently it's not as big a business as over here.

What is true is that we French have specific words and expressions for affairs. But that's only because we're organised. A 5-à-7 (5 till 7 p.m.) is an illicit encounter which usually happens at the end of the afternoon. Some hotels have specific fares for it. A *baise-en-ville* is a small bag you take with you so you can spend the night out without having to come back home.

Affairs have nothing to do with nationality. Well, that's not completely true: you have to give something to the British here, because they invented the very cute concept of the 'fleeting affair'. What does 'fleeting' mean? According to my beloved dictionary, fleeting means 'lasting for a very short time'. As usual, appearances can be deceptive: it's perfectly normal to have a couple of children as a result of a fleeting affair. Hugh Grant has done it, and the fleeting affairs produced at least two kids. I also remember a colleague of mine trying to seduce a young French trainee. He was married with three children but told the trainee that the kids were the result of a fleeting affair. Very fleeting indeed.

What's not to love about a fleeting affair?

Divorcing in London

There's a darker side to London than meets the eye. Over the last few years, London has become the divorce capital of the world. All the oligarchs' wives want to divorce here to maximise their wealth. London has a reputation for protecting the interests of the weaker party (usually, but not always, a wronged wife dumped for a younger version). It's still unclear whether prenups (signed agreements on how the money should be shared in the event of a separation) are valid; either way, from celebrities to bankers' wives, London divorce courts seem to be issuing multimillion-pound settlements every minute. According to the news, the implied message is: if you divorce in London as a woman, you'll be rich.

In theory, this is all good: just look elsewhere if you need some convincing. If reports are to be believed, divorcing in China, for instance, is a nasty business and lots of women have ended up homeless as a result. But an unexpected side effect of this divorce thing is that there's a growing part of the population in London taking advantage of such measures. They're called, unofficially, the 'professional divorcees'. I'm sure you've already met at least one.

Being a professional divorcee is a job. You need to take extremely good care of yourself (a two-hour daily workout is a must, not to mention spa appointments, cosmetic dentistry and surgery, stunning wardrobe, oversized ego …) But the important thing is anticipation. A friend of mine was a successful banker until recession struck. He knew he was going to get sacked at some point and told his then-wife that they would need to tighten their belts a bit. She quickly joined an upmarket dating agency and found herself another rich man before filing for divorce and getting a handsome settlement for, amongst other things, 'emotional distress' – apparently he was working so hard that she was barely seeing him. Six months later, my friend was not only sacked, but also divorced and depressed.

Another acquaintance of mine waited ten years (to the day) in London to file for divorce (they were living in mainland Europe before that). Things hadn't been great for a couple of years. But she calmly explained that she had to wait because after ten years you're sure to be able to apply English common law, which was much more favourable for her (and a lot more expensive for her husband). She ended up with an eight-figure settlement. Her patience paid off.

This made me wonder. The system in the London courts is about 'fairness' and protecting the children as well as the weaker party. But some use and abuse it to maximise their own personal wealth, not understanding that, in doing so, they undermine the credibility of the entire system. But they don't care, because in the short term they'll benefit from it. Maybe it's just an unavoidable side effect of trying too hard to be fair. Or maybe 'what goes around comes around' and eventually the 'professional divorcees' will be taken to the cleaners themselves or end up on their own. Only time will tell.

BAROMETER

Question:
How do you get a British man to express his feelings?

Answers:
1. One pint. (No.)
2. Two pints. (No.)
3. Three pints. (No.)
4. Four pints. (Maybe.)
5. Six pints. (Maybe, but then he has to rush to the loo.)
6. Seven pints. (He's completely drunk and beyond words.)

Question:
What's the latest craze amongst London divorce lawyers?

Answers:
1. A prenup. (No, that's completely out of fashion.)
2. A postnup. (Yes, this is really taking off.)
3. Parental agreements. (Very fashionable indeed.)
4. Decree nisi. (A classic.)
5. Decree absolute. (The holy grail of all divorcees.)

Question:
How do you say you want a quiet evening to your partner?

Answers:

1. Not tonight, darling, I have a headache. (Very French.)
2. How about a nice cup of tea? (Old-generation British.)
3. I'm suffering from a bout of asexuality. (New-generation British.)

WORKING IN THE UK

IS IT WORTH IT?

> *'Work is the curse of the drinking classes.'*
> Oscar Wilde (1854–1900), playwright, novelist, poet

There are many different ways to come and work in the UK. Some privileged employees still today manage to negotiate a very attractive expat package that covers housing, school fees, private healthcare and so on and so forth. You can spot them in the most expensive streets of London because they're always complaining about something. Despite having so much, they can't help it: they have to moan.

I especially try to steer away from French expats after what happened to me the other day. I was trying to write while sipping my cappuccino when two guys entered the coffee shop. They were French, reasonably good-looking and fashionably unshaven. Typical metrosexuals, with Armani jeans and Hollister T-shirts. They believed nobody could understand them. Typical behaviour, isn't it? They sat down and started a passionate conversation about their respective trading positions while sipping their skinny lattes.

Things were not well. The French bankers had the blues.
Taxes were too high, according to them. It wasn't worth staying in London any more. One was considering going back to France, the other felt trapped because his children were going to British schools, but he might consider a move to Singapore. His wife was having her annual health check-up, paid for by the lovely private health insurance. She then had a spa appointment and would pick up the kids later. One of them was going to the Philippines for their holidays (where did they find the time and the money?) Life was clearly super difficult.

Come on, how can you complain when you have so much? How can the rest of us manage if the rich expats can't?

It's all to do with being a glass-half-full sort of person. Everybody works hard and struggles in London, but Londoners usually do it head-on with a smile and without self-pity. We just get on with things. Working in the UK also means being resilient: redundancies are now part of a working career, and are seen as an opportunity to rebound. It's not that big a deal to get sacked any more: it's bound to happen eventually. Over here, 'Success is not final, failure is not fatal: it is the courage to continue that counts.' So Winston Churchill said.

A BRITISH EDUCATION

The Education Act of 1944 introduced free secondary education for all in England and Wales.

That's the theory …

One very good reason to come and work over here is that a British education is one of the best ways for a child to become a confident citizen of the world.

It's entirely possible to live in a bubble in the UK. You might, for instance, enrol your children in a French/German/Swedish school and completely forget that you're living in the UK. However, should you choose to go native, you might find – as I did – that the British system is better suited to well-rounded, generalist children who are eager to learn and discover the world. Don't be fooled by the relaxed atmosphere: selection starts from a very young age.

Tutored to death

The latest fashion in the UK is to hire as many tutors as possible for your kids. I hadn't realised how widespread this trend was until I volunteered to help my daughter and a group of friends to do a school project. It was impossible to meet up because one of the girls had a tutor for each subject. When we finally managed to go to her place, we had to wait for tutor number one to finish. We then worked on the project, and the next tutor was already there, waiting in the living room, when we left. The girl in question was seven. Yes, seven!

I'm not going to patronise anyone and say that you shouldn't tutor your kids because it's a personal choice, each to their own and all that. Often, teachers say you shouldn't do it. My children once had a headmistress who said to the whole school during assembly that 'she hated tutors'. She was running a successful tutoring business on the side. She was doing some parents a favour, wasn't she. Talk about British double standards.

Why do some parents tutor their kids to death? I know it's a competitive world out there, but come on, kids need to have a life. As I'm not British born, I pay attention to my daughter's schoolwork myself. That still makes me a pushy mum, I suppose. But surely tutoring your own kids is fine? I'm not saying I might not fall in with the British tutoring obsession and hire a tutor at some point, but it's not my first thought.

Getting it right

As much as I like the British way of always being positive and never saying 'no', I still feel very French when telling my children that they're wrong when they've made a mistake. Let me explain: I was looking at one of my daughter's maths tests (she was eight at the time). On one of the questions, the answer was £1.60. She had answered £1.75. In my eyes, her answer was wrong; the question was just a basic calculation.

In France, the teacher would have put a red cross and written 'Wrong'. Not over here. The teacher had put 'Almost correct' and given her half a mark. I couldn't believe it. Is there such a thing as being 'almost correct'? I didn't think there was. Clearly, I was wrong.

My daughter was very happy to have got it 'almost' right. I wasn't. She clearly thought I was a grumpy old woman. Correction: a strict mum. If the school was happy, why wouldn't I be? One of maths' specificities is that you can't have it 'almost right'. It's either right or wrong. When, in a shop, you're given your change back, it's correct or it isn't. Period.

What does being 'almost right' mean anyway? How can you progress and do better next time if you're told that you were 'almost correct'? Kids (and adults also) need to know what went wrong in order to learn from their mistakes. Making mistakes and failing is pretty normal. And it's not that big a deal. The sooner you learn from your mistakes, the better. How can you do this if you're not corrected? Why are people afraid, in this country, to correct kids?

I am not saying that we should focus all the time on children's mistakes. I'm just saying that mistakes need to be corrected in order to move on to the next level. That's all.

I know life isn't black and white. I know that, sometimes, the difference between success and failure is tiny. But surely it doesn't mean that being 'almost correct' is 'good enough'. Or am I wrong?

Does it all add up?

When, aged seven, my elder daughter didn't know her two times tables, my (French) husband thought she had a learning difficulty. To be fair to him, she also wasn't able to solve simple problems, such as a pear costs 70p and an apple 60p, how much do two pears and one apple cost? There were huge rows at home between the two of them and I ended up suggesting that we see a child psychologist to defuse the situation. My hope was that it would calm things down. My daughter was duly assessed and the eminent psychologist told us that she was absolutely fine, and we were too pushy. It was we who had a problem, not her.

We were baffled. Eventually we understood that, unlike in France, the British education is not based on maths. Quite the opposite. I keep hearing about hot-air balloon debates and 'show and tell'. If you don't know your times tables, it's not a big deal over here. It is in France, where the selections are almost exclusively based on your level of maths. No wonder I keep noticing that the amount of change I get after a purchase is often wrong. The British can't add up!

In France, the emphasis on pure maths is unbelievable, and starts at a young age. I learned about topology at thirteen. Yes, thirteen. And no, you don't want to know about it. Suffice to know, I once talked to an American PhD maths student at Harvard and she didn't know what it was.

Despite such a great academic education, I have yet to see more Frenchmen high up in the commercial, industrial or political hierarchy. I'm pretty sure there are exceptions, but my point is that, given that we have to learn so much about maths, quantum physics, philosophy, Latin and the like, why don't we have more French men or women at the top of the tree in all the big global companies?

Maybe, despite all its failings, the British system has got something right: the curriculum is more balanced and builds the children's confidence in a very effective way.

Boarding school

A very British invention. Here, when your kids are seven, you can ship them off to a boarding school. This means that you're only going to see them during weekends – if you're lucky – or during holidays, if they're not holidaying with their friends.

This is the main reason why British people tend to have only one child if they're not insanely rich. Because, for the privilege of not seeing your child any more, you'll have to fork out more than £3,500 a month. Yes, you read that right.

Apparently, boarding schools are back in fashion. My daughter, at one point, desperately wanted to go to one because all her British friends wanted to. It made my French blood boil. The phase passed, which is good – and the upshot was that we didn't have to remortgage the house.

I asked one of her classmates why she wanted to go. She answered that 'it was going to help her independence'. I was gobsmacked. She was ten. I must have missed a trick.

What is the impact of going to boarding school? It depends. Most kids seem to survive, find themselves and even thrive, but some become emotionally damaged for a long, long time. Going to boarding school shapes you for life. It leaves subtle marks: a certain distance when you speak to others, a will to perfection in everything you do, a fierce independence mixed with extreme vulnerability, and a sense of having been through something – a real accomplishment. Oh, and most boarding schools are single sex. I'm convinced that it might explain why over here so many men are into cross-dressing. Weird. As for girls, some end up traumatised and find it difficult to trust anyone.

To be fair, most of the time it's not too bad for the kids. But for all French mums the result is the same: lots of tears, and anti-depressants eventually. Wine might help. Some friends of mine started drinking in their forties, when their kids left for boarding school. In order to cope, they had to spend more money in their fifties on rehab, cleaning up their act. They ended up almost broke, and sometimes single. Tough.

A lot of Brits want to make it look like they went to a posh and expensive boarding school when they didn't. It's a game of pretence. One day they're all posh; the next they're chewing gum and swearing as if there's no tomorrow. Why can't they just accept who they are?

As for me, I would only send my children to boarding school if I had no choice, perhaps if I were sick, or living far from a city. Call me a French mum!

HOW TO FIND A JOB AND GET PROMOTED

'It is better to fail in originality than to succeed in imitation'
Herman Melville (1819–1891), American novelist

If you want to find a job, you made the right move when you came to the UK. Urban legend says that most French students who can't find jobs in their home country are able to work as soon as they get off the Eurostar, just by asking cafés and restaurants whether they need any help.

If you're after a more qualified job, though, you'll have to overcome a few hurdles, including having the right attitude. Here are a few tips:

The stiff upper lip

If you're upset, you're not supposed to show it. The proper attitude is to keep a stiff upper lip and pretend that you're fine with whatever has happened, even if you've just been made redundant. Then you go to the pub and get properly sloshed. That's the correct etiquette, in Britain, for dealing with any sort of work problem.

Christmas parties
Now, repeat after me: what happens at the Christmas party stays at the Christmas party. One day, a former boss of mine ended up being so drunk that he started riding the fire extinguisher and hitting on all his female colleagues. Nobody said anything the following day. He acted perfectly normally and it was business as usual. There was an elephant in the room but we weren't allowed to talk about it.

Sounding educated
It is a truth universally acknowledged over here that if you want to impress your interlocutors you need to use French words and expressions when you speak. But when I do it, my British colleagues don't understand. This is because they pronounce French words the British way. We French usually stress the last syllable in French, whereas the British seem to love stressing the first one. They usually don't get what I'm saying. To add insult to injury, they often write French words with spelling mistakes. Pain au Chocolat will become Pain au Chocolate and savoir faire savoirfair. I don't bother correcting them. I just smile.

Don't fight the stereotypes
Embrace them and turn them to your advantage. For instance, the perception that French women are sexy is deeply entrenched in the British mind. I've never understood why; I suppose that's just

the way it is. It's probably better for French women (yes, that would be me too) to exploit such a preconception rather than fight it. So yes, apparently we have a certain *je ne sais quoi* and a fragility that looks sexy. I had no idea that I had it, but it comes with the passport, evidently. Use it to negotiate a discount with your heavy French accent, or get a freebie, or even a salary increase. There is no point in explaining that I happen to be a Signalling Engineer, and that I don't do glamour – I need to pick my battles and this one is not worth fighting.

Talk the talk

You need to know how to make a good presentation and get the right messages across. I used to write down useful words and expressions so I could reuse them. Until one day I found out about a very useful website called Corporate Bullshit Generator – just google it. Oh, and I ended setting up my own business, which helped too because I was no longer dependent on making the right impression on my bosses.

Understate, understate, understate

Boasting about a major achievement is looked down upon. I'll always remember the newly appointed CEO of a major company saying that he just 'got lucky'. He was brilliant and hard-working. Luck had nothing to do with it.

SETTING UP A BUSINESS

'Any time is a good time to start a company.'
Ron Conway (b.1951), angel investor

After a decade in London, I've come to the conclusion that most French have tip-top academic training but very limited business acumen. We're not taught how to do business when we study. I was led to believe that, if I were ever to set up a business, it would have to be in a complicated field such as statistical physics. A bit of a narrow field, perhaps? It had never occurred to me that a business could be simple and still make money. There is, in France, some sort of intellectual snobbery when you talk about a 'normal' business. Things have to be complicated. Or you have to be a civil servant. Being a civil servant and having a job for life is the ultimate sign of success. If you do something complicated and are a civil servant, then you've hit the jackpot (within the French intellectual hierarchy, at least).

But don't think we French are nerds. Far from it. Most of us are charming and very well educated. We can sustain a conversation on every possible subject. We like to have original views. We're capable of a very high level of intellectual abstraction. But we aren't usually very pragmatic. That's simply not our forte.

That's why setting up a business in France is so complicated that most of us pay a lawyer or an accountant to do it. And to top everything off, it takes at least two or three weeks to get your company registration number. And after that you'll discover taxes that you didn't even know existed.

Setting up in the UK

Things are slightly different over here, and you can do pretty much everything by post or on the Internet. Oh, and the Brits have all sorts of help lines. Don't bother calling them, though: they never work. After a 30-minute wait you'll be told that the lines are busy and could you please check their website? Simply charming. If you're willing to pay a few thousand pounds, I'm pretty sure that there will be a fast track system somewhere. Because there always is.

On the bright side, setting up a business over here is pretty straightforward and can be done from the comfort of your own place. I told you, the Brits are far more pragmatic. The same goes with passports, driving licences and various other formalities. Everything is far easier in Britain.

As an example, I had wanted a second French passport for quite some time because it wasn't working any more. Every time I went abroad I was sent to a special counter because the magnetic strip wasn't recognised and they needed to check it manually, which always took ages. I think my passport was trying to tell me something: it had gone on strike.

I went to the French consulate to get a second one, only to be told that I needed loads of additional documents, such as my work contract. It felt a bit like being told off by a Stasi officer in the old German Democratic Republic. Big Brother was watching me. I needed to give out all my secrets. I didn't. I paid £25 to get an additional British passport and it arrived within twenty-four hours. No questions asked. I'm not sure I'll renew my French passport when it expires. I'm too scared of all the questions I'll have to answer.

Better here than there

So having been brought up in France, I thought that a business had to be complicated, involve quantum physics and necessitated at least a couple of PhDs. I had no idea that a business could not only be simple but also make life easier.

I've discovered a completely different business culture this side of the Channel. From mumpreneurs to teenagers who create all sorts of successful apps, businesses are everywhere, and it's difficult not to catch the entrepreneurial bug over here. There are plenty of extremely successful British business ventures, such as Virgin, Asos or Hailo. If you have a good business idea in London, the sky's the limit.

If you have a good idea in France, the whole world and its sister will come after you to ask for as much money as possible. I'm talking from experience here: when I wanted to expand my business there, I quickly found out that I would end up earning less because of a very French double whammy: my tax rate would jump, and I would have to pay the new rate on the capital of the loan I was reimbursing each month. To cut a long story short, it wasn't worth it. And don't forget the huge number of forms you'll have to fill in.

BAROMETER

Question:
How long does it take to set up a company in the UK?

Answers:
1. Three weeks with the help of a lawyer. (Just admit you're French.)
2. 5 minutes on the Internet. (Yes, it is possible.)

Question:
How do you get into a faith school in the UK?

Answers:
1. If you're not religious, you convert.
2. Go to church every Sunday.
3. Get to know the priest/minister.
4. If you don't believe it, fake it.
5. All of the above. (Right answer. It's a lot of work, and it's extremely competitive.)

BRITISH CULTURE AND VALUES

SOME THINGS YOU SHOULD KNOW

> 'The battle of Waterloo was won on the playing fields of Eton.'
> Arthur Wellesley, aka 1st Duke of Wellington (1769–1852),
> soldier and statesman

In order to practise your 'life in the UK' test to get your citizenship, you should know about the main battles that the British have won. In your daily life, you'll be reminded at every possible opportunity about such battles. Don't bother too much to learn about the ones the British have lost.

We French also have a selective historical memory: we were also mainly taught about the battles that France had won. I belong to a generation of students that never, ever heard about Napoleon. For some reason it wasn't mentioned in the history manuals. I understand that things are different in the UK because most of my British friends are experts on the Napoleonic wars. Apparently they had to learn about Napoleon over and over again. They're always shocked when I don't understand their allusions to this part of our shared history. (For the record, I really, *really* don't understand them.)

I can't work out if this was why I was once given a lovely lecture by some well-meaning colleagues. A real crash course on the Napoleonic wars. One day everybody from the accounting department crammed into my office to re-enact the Battle of Waterloo. They had brought me a present: a Napoleonic bicorne hat.

"You have to wear it all day, it's our office tradition. And you're the only French citizen in the office today, so wear it with pride!'

What was wrong with everybody? Why did they care so much about Waterloo? It reminded me that whatever it seemed like to me, for my colleagues, whatever I did, I would always be French, with or without my British passport.

Mind the steps

I've always liked London. I don't know why. Maybe it's because of the energy, the various parks and the narrow, cobbled streets. Or perhaps it's because London has all the ingredients of organised chaos.

Take Paris, for instance. Someone called Haussmann decided, in the middle of the 19th century, to renovate and reorganise Paris. Old individual houses were destroyed and the main streets were completely rebuilt, boasting tall, modern buildings and wide avenues. It was all about 'order' and ensuring consistency of style.

As a result, if one day you have to move to Paris and can't afford to buy a *Hotel Particulier* (in other words a big, posh house) in the XVIth district, you will soon find out that it's virtually impossible to buy a house in Paris at all.

Things are different in London. Buying a house doesn't come cheap, but remains possible. Lots of streets still have terraced houses, some Victorian, others Georgian. The capital is made up of different layers and hasn't had to sustain a heavy programme of renovation over the last 250 years. It shows. It makes it more human.

This means that my old Victorian house is full of steps. To be precise, there are eighty-seven of them in total. You have the whole story now, with facts and figures, so don't complain, please. Most old houses in London have lots of steps. We simply get used to it. And the silver lining is that we exercise without even thinking about it. Climbing up and down the stairs make our bottoms a lot firmer, didn't you know? It doesn't bother me at all. You know what: I like it. Each floor is quite isolated from the rest of the house and it's easy to spend time together on one floor, or to have some private time on another floor.

What still bothers me is all the comments I have to listen to when family and (French) friends come over. I can be sure that they'll complain about all the steps. Maybe complaining is part of the French culture. It's only a matter of time before someone asks about the stairs. It usually takes a drink or two and then the complaining squad starts firing.

Sometimes, it's a criticism hidden within concern for my family:

'Aren't you afraid to fall, with all the steps?'

'What about your children?'

We've never fallen so far, and it's been almost fourteen years now.

My mother is especially good at making complaints and reproaches in a seemingly helpful way:

'It would be great if you could have everything on the same level in a flat. It would feel so much bigger.'

'If you ask me, the lounge should be on the same floor as the dining room.'

The thing is, nobody's asking her.

Such comments drive me mad. Not to mention the fact that London service charges are rocket-high for flats, and in a house you're less likely to hear your upstairs/downstairs neighbours. But no, the complaining squad doesn't want to see all the positive sides of living in a house. They have to make their point, even if nobody asks them to.

Here's the thought that crossed my mind last time I had such a comment: if the worst comes to the worst, I'll push them down the stairs. I'm sure they'll be delighted to be right: stairs are so dangerous.

Cultural icons

The red telephone box and the red Royal Mail postbox are spread throughout the UK and are cultural icons. But don't get your hopes up: nowadays, the main use for red telephone boxes is for prostitutes to advertise their services. Postboxes, you'll be pleased to know, can still be used to send letters.

The British have their own icons, such as the BBC, double-decker buses, Big Ben and the Royal Family (and of course this list isn't exhaustive).
Icons are what keep the British nation together, and their importance shouldn't be overlooked. The British, just like the French, have their own language, and their own icons. Get with it.

Literature

It all comes down to Shakespeare.

Be prepared: you'll have to read, study, and breathe Shakespeare. You'll be told that Shakespeare wrote the greatest stories of all time, that he changed history and so on and so forth. Shakespeare is the main author your children will study if you decide to send them to a British school. This obsession with Shakespeare never ends. Because everything derives from Shakespeare.

BEHAVING BRITISH

> *'I am at heart a gentleman.'*
> Marlene Dietrich (1901–1992), actress and singer

The values and principles of the UK can be summarised as follows:

- Behave morally and ethically
- Treat each other with fairness and respect
- Behave responsibly

So that's the theory. Things are slightly different in practice.

As an example, it's my lot in life to be mocked for my bad English accent. In London, especially during business meetings, you can be sure that, when I say something, some condescending chap will take a few seconds to answer me back, as if he (it's usually a he, I must admit) needs some time to process my French accent and understand what on earth I'm saying. Usually they put on a look of concentration, eyes half closed, and lean their ear slightly closer to me. I absolutely hate it and can feel my blood boiling when they do that. The curious thing is that most people have absolutely no problem getting what I say. Go figure.

British men also think that their sense of humour is extremely funny, and I've heard countless times that 'she's a bit stressed – she must be on her period'. Ah-ah. When I pointed out that it was a sexist comment, they looked incredulous and thought I was mad.

When it comes to it, if you're not treated as you should be, you can always threaten to report the culprit for discrimination. It should solve the problem immediately.

The British sense of humour

The British sense of humour might be baffling at first.

Come to think of it, the British sense of humour is a minefield.

I'm pretty sure we've all been in similar situations: you're on a date with a reasonably good-looking bloke, and then he feels comfortable enough to crack a joke. But you don't find it funny at all. For instance, I don't get Monty Python jokes. This is because I was brought up in France. When a guy starts quoting Monty Python and laughing out loud, I feel like yawning. I don't get it, and even if I'm trying, I just can't see the humour in it. Seriously, what's so hilarious about mimicking the sound of a horse's gallop? To be honest with you, I find it incredibly boring. Some guys also still indulge in jokes about blondes. Everybody knows that such jokes have long passed their sell-by date.

I'm trying to say that we all have a slightly different sense of humour. Some of it might even relate to your nationality, your gender or your education.

Here are a few examples to better illustrate my point:

- We French love to laugh at somebody else's expense. We rarely do self-deprecation. We need a target. When we find one, and we tend to be great teases, we're often perceived to be arrogant and rude. So much for trying to be funny.
- The British believe that everybody loves fancy-dress parties. What they don't know is that tarts and vicar parties aren't that big a hit abroad. Enough said!
- Of course Germans have a sense of humour. But remember that they don't really do stand-up comedy.
- I have to say that a lot of Frenchmen love to joke about subjects that would upset most Americans, like ethnicity, gender, family, fidelity, and, yes, they also love earthy jokes about sex and bodily functions. I can only hope the British don't hold it against them. The funny thing is that we Frenchwomen don't much enjoy such jokes. Go figure.
- Unlike their French neighbours, Italians have been mocking each other ferociously for more than two thousand years.

So what should you do? Should you nod nicely when someone cracks a joke that you don't find funny at all, or should you stand up and leave? You need to think carefully about this one, because it might not be entirely the other person's fault. In my view, you need to gently explain that you didn't really warm up to the joke. The trouble is, some people absolutely have to prove that they're funny, and instead of backing off and changing the subject, they'll make it their new purpose in life to convince you that you're an old bore because you didn't laugh at their joke. 'Oh, come on, it is funny. You're so stuck-up not to laugh. Let your hair down, I don't *really* mean it, but … '

You can't win. Just smile and nod.

How to complain

It's easy once you know how to do it: understate, understate, understate. Then repeat until the other person gets it. Because over here, if you want to be heard or taken seriously, there's no point in being blunt – it's not going to serve you well. You have to tackle the matter in a tactful, indirect way. You need to take baby steps and slowly get to your point. I know it can be frustrating, but this is the only way you'll have a chance of making things happen. Just a chance.

For instance, you're simply not supposed to state the bare facts. One of my friends lost a significant amount of blood and almost passed away while giving birth to her daughter. She wasn't too pleased about how the hospital had handled the whole situation. Her comment about the whole experience was: 'It stung a little bit, I suppose.' I was gobsmacked. She'd almost died. My other English friends nodded. They all understood what she meant. Clearly, I needed to learn.

I've tried again and again to complain the British way, but it's been a steep learning curve.

I once set up a meeting with a client, and my junior colleague showed up forty-five minutes late, unshaven, and smelling like fish. Not to mention that his hair looked like a battlefield.

How could I complain about his unacceptable attitude and convey the message that this was not acceptable?

In France, I would have sent him back home. Pure and simple. With some harsh words such as: 'Get yourself sorted! Your behaviour is not acceptable in a professional environment. This is a final warning … '

Over here, I wasn't so sure. How could I tackle the issue? I decided to put my observations into practice. I took him outside the meeting room and said something like, 'I see you had a bit of a blooper this morning. Would you please go and wash and we'll talk about this later?' He nodded and did what I said.

A couple of months later, and despite all my tactful explanations about how to behave in a corporate environment, he fell asleep during a business meeting. To this day I'm still wondering whether the French approach would have worked better.

How do the Brits do it? How do they get things done while practising the art of understatement? I sometimes wonder.

Point scorers and how to manage them

In the UK, people like to score points on a daily basis. At work. With friends. Down the pub. Point scorers are simply everywhere. It's probably got something to do with a love of debating and talking. They just love to show off.

Don't get me wrong; in France too there are point scorers. But somehow, over there, saying 'I don't know' in a business meeting is often seen as honest (as long as you don't keep saying it). Not here. It's your job to know. Or rather, it's your job to make it look like you know.

The point scorer will start talking in a meeting even if he or she has nothing to say. (S)he will have to make a point during the first five minutes of the meeting, because they can't help it.

The point scorer feels like they know everything. They've done it all, they've seen it all. And even if it's not the case, they'll have a strong opinion about it. Basically, they know it all and they let you know it. How to deal with point scorers is part of your survival kit in London.

So how do you spot them?

They're everywhere. It's the driver behind you who's going to start honking madly when your car has just stopped while you're changing gear because you're in a difficult position. (Honking will not help me. Quite the opposite. I'm dealing with the issue, thank you very much. Just give me ten seconds. Surely you can stay calm for ten seconds?)

It's the work colleague who keeps talking and doesn't do anything. They'll be the first one to notice that you're late, while they 'work from home' every Friday.

It's the boss who likes lecturing everyone. They often use expressions like 'In my opinion', 'If you ask me … '. Nobody asks them.

They love talking about themselves. 'When I was working in Tanzania … ' In fact they spent a two-week holiday there. A good test is to stop talking or stop doing what you're doing and see whether they continue their diatribe. It usually works very well.

There's no point explaining that no, you know better because you happen to have some real experience on the subject. The point scorer doesn't listen anyway and will make a point of having the last word. If you have to use words, you have to be brief and hit hard. Go for the kill. You need to say something like 'This is completely wrong' and be able to prove it simply.

I personally believe that actions speak louder than words. I usually shut up and, as they seem to know better, I carefully avoid working with them on specific subjects. I let them deal with it on their own, with very clear deadlines if possible.

When a honking driver is trying to make a point, I drive even more slowly. I don't get angry or swear. I act. They can't fly over me.

The plus of being a point scorer is that they're too silly to question themselves. I believe this must make them immune to mental illnesses such as breakdowns. They don't doubt, you see.

Now you're warned. In my view, the best way to deal with point scorers is to get a life and do what you enjoy, no matter what. As we say in French, 'the dogs bark, but the caravan goes on'.

Sport and fair play

Over here, I've found out about sports I didn't even know existed, such as cricket and netball. And I've learnt that, in all sports, fair play is supposed to prevail. It involves treating everyone equally and impartially. It's also understood to mean using only tactics that are in accord with the spirit of the game. Behind this façade, however, the British are as competitive as the rest of us.

I need to come clean here: I don't get cricket. I hope the British authorities won't retain my passport because I've just told you this!

Let me explain. First of all, I've never understood the rules. When does the match start? When does it finish? I have absolutely no idea. Then again, it doesn't matter because the whole thing can last up to three days. My knowledge is limited to the fact that there is some batting and bowling involved. No contact. No fights. Apparently, there's a good chance you'll be having a cup of tea while the only action of the day is happening. Maybe cricket is just an excuse to drink and socialise? I'm also told that cricket players have a lot of success with women. I wonder why that is. I don't see that they have a thing about them. Simply put, they don't do it for me. But during the Ashes, all your British colleagues will be in front of their screen.

I much prefer rugby. I love watching the players and their strong bodies. (OK, and especially their muscular rears, I admit it.) They fight, they sweat, and the game is full of testosterone. Rugby is a contact game and I totally get it. I understand what tries and penalties are about, and also that a converted try can be worth seven points. And even if I don't get all the rules, I enjoy watching the players. To me, the rugby player is the epitome of manhood: he can fight and get dirty but he has to follow some rules – he's not someone you want to challenge. What's not to love about them?

Sticks and stones

Even when things get rough, over here you're supposed to keep a dignified attitude. As the saying goes, 'Sticks and stones might break my bones, but words will never hurt me.' Enough said.

CUSTOMS, IDIOSYNCRASIES AND THE WIDER WORLD

BRITISH WAYS

> *'Very few of us are what we seem.'*
> Agatha Christie (1890–1976), English crime novelist

Boxing Day

In France, we don't celebrate Boxing Day. We simply don't have it. The British would find this really, really tough, but it's true. It's common practice to go back to work on the 26th of December. Usually, we celebrate Christmas on Christmas Eve and have a big lunch on the 25th. That's it, celebrations over. See – contrary to popular belief, the French are sometimes still working when the Anglo-Saxon world just stops for a massive shopping spree! I thought I should clarify this difference. Somehow it makes me feel better. It might have something to do with the fact that I used to be told all the time that 'we French' never work.

When we first moved to London, I didn't understand why you don't have to go to work on the 26th of December. It took me a while to get it. Boxing Day is just a bonus for me. As long as you avoid the long queues at all the shops, London is empty and it's a good time to catch up with family and just take it easy.

Bank holiday or public holiday?

After more than fourteen years in this country, I'm still struggling to understand the difference between a bank holiday and a public holiday. Everybody has a different interpretation. I've now come to the conclusion that it's the exact same thing. It seems that when discussing bank or public holidays, the ultimate goal is to confuse you, to show you don't understand how this country works. It's a secret code the British use to make fun of foreigners.

You'll get long-winded explanations about the fact that public holidays are supposed to be religious festivals, like Christmas or Easter, and bank holidays are supposed to be the rest. Apparently, the August bank holiday was initially for bank clerks only, hence the term 'bank' holiday. You'll be told that Christmas is a public holiday, and so is Boxing Day. But shouldn't Boxing Day be a bank holiday if it's not a religious festival? I don't get it.

I suspect that some aspects of life over here will always be a mystery to me. That's the beauty of living in a different country, I suppose.

I'm not going to stress about it: bank holiday or public holiday you don't have to go to work. Who cares about the difference?

Sending cards

What do you do in London when you want to be polite but not too involved? You just send a card. There's a card for every possible opportunity. Over here, you can find Christmas cards, Easter cards, Valentine's Day cards, I'm-sorry-you're-leaving-cards, thank-you cards, bar mitzvah cards, birthday cards, baptism cards, wedding cards, and I'm sure I'm forgetting most of them …

In France, we don't have such a culture of sending cards at every possible opportunity. If you care for someone, you just talk to this person. Or you call. Or you send a real letter – or, as times have changed, an email, but a personalised one. The only formal occasion when you're required to send a card would be at the start of the year – we French don't do Christmas cards, we do Happy New Year cards.

Initially I thought this habit of sending cards was nice. Now I'm not so sure. You can be awful to someone and then send an I'm-sorry card. It's not even necessary to write anything in the card. You just have to sign and send. You can add a few words – something as vague as "you're a very special person" – and that should do the trick.

Surely if you care about the person you're sending a card to, you'd try to make more of an effort? Come to think of it, maybe that's the whole point: you don't send a card to people you truly care about, do you?

Over time, I grew tired of cards. I believe that most of the cards I've received have been some kind of hypocritical excuse for pretending that the senders care about me or my family, given to me to avoid a conversation, or more direct contact, or simply because it looked polite and they didn't know what to say. Most of them ended up in the bin right away. Having said that, I've kept a few, because they were genuinely nice and referred to something I could relate to.

Usually, I have to force myself to reply to cards. I know it's supposed to be polite, but I feel I'm just perpetuating a tradition I don't like.

Sending cards over here is an art. It has to be the right card (for obvious reasons you can't send a happy birthday card when you're meant to send a Christmas card), and, if possible, should include something "witty".

So, where did it all go wrong? When did people start to box relationships into cards? I totally need to design an 'I don't send any cards' card. I would make a fortune.

Manners
Since we moved over here, I've learned of many manners I never knew existed – or cared about, for that matter. But good manners are the key here. I'm convinced you could get away with murder provided you were well mannered. And you'd need to be charming and polite as well. Words definitely matter. Actions sometimes don't seem to. It's style over substance. You can say the meanest things while being polite and pretending to be nice.

For example, I once had to wait a good ten minutes to get my much-needed cappuccino because the barista was busy chatting away with her colleague. Busy night, apparently – good for her, but none of my business. When she eventually realised that there was a long queue, and after at least ten failed attempts on my part to grab her attention, she politely said, 'Sorry to keep you waiting, darling,' and then smiled.

What she meant was: 'I couldn't care less about you guys – I had important things to say, and come on, you can wait a little bit for your posh coffee, can't you?'

I didn't smile back as I was slightly annoyed. I'm not in a good mood before my first coffee.

She then asked: 'Skinny or normal, your cappuccino?'

I was outraged. I had my coffee here every morning. What she probably meant was: 'Haven't you put a bit of weight on lately?'

I couldn't believe it.

'No, full fat as usual, please.'

What I meant was: 'As you can see, I don't need to diet and you know perfectly well what I want as I come here every morning.'

I think she got the point. I might change coffee shop anyway.

And more than once I've applied for jobs I didn't get. I remember calling the secretary of one of the companies I'd applied to in order to try to understand why I hadn't got the job. The response I had was nothing short of astounding.

'You didn't expect to get the job, darling, did you?'

This means: 'You knew you were too thick to get the job, surely.'

It's the way Brits are educated from a very early age. You have to conform and be polite in all circumstances. My younger daughter didn't get into a posh nursery in London because at her assessment – when she was three – she finished her scribbles, got bored and started to pull her little friend's (very nice and expensive) dress. This is not acceptable behaviour, I gather, even at three, if you want to become a lady – which, after careful consideration, I'm not sure I want for my daughters.

French can be a lot blunter, and it felt nice, at first, to be surrounded by seemingly polite people. Now I'm not so sure.

Good manners are relative. What's considered to be polite over here might be rude in a different country. As an example, if you're invited to dinner at 7.30 p.m. in France, you're not expected before 8 p.m. Should you arrive on time, you might have to witness the delivery of the so-called home-made meal by the local caterer. Very rude indeed and you won't get invited again.

Even within Britain, good manners can be different from one family to another. Don't you think that good manners are all about being flexible and respecting each other? This means that I'll eat with my right hand when invited by my Indian friends, and with silver cutlery when I have a posh lunch at the Wolseley.

Occasionally, I get it completely wrong. I once patted my friend's son's head, not knowing that as they're Indonesian you're not meant to do this: the head is supposed to be where the soul rests. My friends didn't insult me, they just explained it to me – they knew I didn't mean to be rude. We moved on and got on with our lives.

This leads me to my second point: do these well-mannered people have a life? Do they have real-life problems – you know, as in health issues, relationship issues, real work projects. Good manners for the sake of them is, I believe, pointless.

Apparently, I've missed something.

Queuing

An unofficial sport this side of the Channel is queuing. You have to do it everywhere: at the post office, while waiting for a Tube or a bus, at your surgery and so on ... There's a proper etiquette to queuing. You need to be patient, courteous and maybe smile or nod, especially if you think you know someone in the queue. Your manners, once again, need to be impeccable in all circumstances, even if you're short of time or it's pouring with rain or the guy in front of you stinks because he's completely drunk. Anyone who tries to jump the queue will be told something like, 'Excuse me, dear, the queue is over here – you need to get in line.'

Don't try to be like this in France, especially in cities like Paris or Marseille, otherwise you're going to spend the whole day wherever you're queuing. As far as queuing is concerned, we French have no rules. Instead of thinking, 'Let's be gracious and wait for it to be over,' our mindset is 'How can I cut this queue?'

The British wouldn't stand a chance if they tried to queue in France, at the French consulate or anywhere remotely French. They don't get how it works: that you don't know anyone, and if you do, you just pretend you don't. All excuses are good to cut the queue, and whoever dares wins. Be very self-assured when you do it, otherwise someone will notice that you're a bit hesitant and will shout at you, and might even insult you. Pretend you don't care. This is all going to be very hard for any British queueing in France, but they just need to be flexible about it and suck it up.

The skill is in making it look like it's OK. Saying something like, 'Excuse me, but I have an appointment,' while looking really stern. It usually works. And if it doesn't, you need to employ a few slang words to reinforce your point – something like *'Bordel, t'es en carafe ou quoi? Je dois y aller fissa!'* (which translates roughly as 'What the hell, are you stuck to the floor or something? Get a move on!' But this far exceeds the Brits' rudeness threshold). Be careful, slang words might not be the same in Marseille as in Paris, and it's important to get it right. There's no point feeling bad about anything said or done to you; it's not personal, and it'll be done to you countless times anyway.

You've got to love the British politeness. This morning I saw a lady in her car, thinking that there was a traffic jam and waiting patiently to be able to move again. On closer inspection, I saw that all the cars in front of her were just parked in line. She seemed baffled because all the traffic lights were green but her line wasn't moving an inch. Dear oh dear! I wonder if she's still there. I'll have a look this evening, just in case.

As for me, I feel like I'm now suffering from a mild form of split personality disorder. As soon as I queue, I assess the type of queue (French or British). It can be a bit complicated – the French queue is coming to London, especially after the last General Election, and the British queue exists in France too (I've seen it a few times. I couldn't believe it). I have to make my decision quick as a flash, and then I behave accordingly. And believe me, I can be ruthless!

Again, I'm trying hard to be flexible and assess the situation.

GPs

If, like me, you're used to the French health system, it will be a steep learning curve. In France, your physician always listens to you. You're always given a prescription, a routine examination, and taken seriously. Your symptoms will never be minimised, and if your doctor has the slightest doubt, you'll be referred for a scan, an X-ray or a blood test. We French also have specific ailments, such as heavy legs or a heavy shoulder, that don't seem to exist on this side of the Channel but are regarded as significant in France.

Over here, the first hurdle, after being registered, is to successfully achieve an appointment. What looks easy in theory is a game of patience and resilience. The line is always busy, and the receptionist will do her utmost to encourage you not to get an appointment, because you're not sick, are you?

After many times calling your practice on speed dial and being hung up on a few times, you might be given a slot, usually two or three days after you need it. Don't believe it's the last of the hurdles you'll have to overcome. It's just the start.

Once you get to see your GP (that's what they call their doctor over here. It stands for General Practitioner), which usually happens after a long wait in the waiting room, you need to convince him or her that you need help. Most of the time, you'll be told to come back in forty-eight hours to see if you feel better, and maybe to take some Nurofen in the meantime. Helpful advice (yes, even we French do sarcasm sometimes). He/she will not examine you at all, because he/she will type on the computer during the whole consultation without looking up. Do not listen to your GP. Keep on complaining until he/she gives up, because you must make it very clear that you're not going to leave without a prescription/a referral/whatever you need – a very useful tactic developed by a friend of mine.

Another surprise was to find that you need to book one appointment for each symptom. This means that, in theory, if both your ears and your throat hurt, you need two appointments. I wonder whether you have to book the whole day to get a full examination?

When I didn't know I was pregnant and was feeling nauseous, I went to see my GP. He spent half of the ten-minute session telling me off because my back was hurting a bit, and I should therefore have made two appointments instead of one. That's when I puked on his desk and collapsed. It got his attention.

Still today, after all these years, I wonder if you'd get a GP to help you if you were on the verge of dying. If you're lucky, they might give you an appointment a couple of days after you've died. And you'll never get to see a GP in the evening or during weekends. You have to be sick during working hours, stupid! This means that, if you need medical attention, you have three options:

1. Jump on the first Eurostar and see a French GP.
2. Go private if you can afford it.
3. Go to your nearest A&E hospital and be prepared to spend a day or two there.

Let's tell it as it is: it looks like the whole system is built for GPs and not for patients. I received a lot of abuse when I first said this, and my response has always been the same: go and see what's happening in other countries and you'll understand where I'm coming from.

Giving birth

You can give birth at home, in a unit run by midwives (a midwifery unit or birth centre) or in a hospital. Some hospitals have a separate midwifery unit. The choice you have about where to have your baby will depend on your needs and risks and, to some extent, on where you live. Wherever you choose, the place should feel right for you.

Wherever you are, remember that this is not France. Expect to 'talk through your pain' and describe how it feels in excruciating detail. And of course expect to be back home in no time.

I'll always remember the birth of my second daughter. I was in pain. I was at the maternity hospital's reception desk. I was told that I needed to be assessed to see whether the birth was imminent or whether I should go back home. The nurse was about to start reading out a questionnaire.

A contraction arrived and I started screaming.

'Perhaps I'll show you to your room.'

Good, I'd passed the assessment with flying colours. I was always good at assessments. It's my thing.

Then I was given a lecture because apparently I should have called before turning up. I snapped back, 'Next time I'll send a fax'. She shut up.

I was then told to 'talk through my pain'. I ended up doing so much more than talking: I shouted, insulted, begged and threatened (not necessarily in that order). I was told to behave myself and to stop screaming, which only made me shout louder and become angrier at the whole world.

In the end there were no complications and I heard the cry of a healthy baby only three hours after having checked in. In France, my body would have been pumped up with chemicals. You've got to love British efficiency!

THE BIGGER PICTURE

*'Whoever speaks of Europe is wrong:
it is a geographical expression.'*
Otto von Bismarck (1815-1898), first chancellor of Germany

Europe

The UK didn't join the European Economic Community (EEC) until 1973. Today, it's still a sore subject. You'll not read anything about the EEC in all the official preparation guides for your citizenship test. No questions on this subject will be asked. There is absolutely no need whatsoever to revise what Europe is about if you want to become British. This is because the British are torn between three worlds:

- Their special relationship with the United States
- The Commonwealth
- The European Union

They're trying to keep everyone happy, but it's difficult.

I walked past the Lithuanian embassy in Pimlico the other day with an American friend of mine. There was a long queue outside. Despite being an educated lady, she started a racist rant about the fact that 'these people' – meaning the Eastern Europeans – had more rights than she did in the European Union in general, and in the UK in particular. What a shame it was, she said. I couldn't believe it. Isn't America a land of immigrants, I thought? She probably didn't realise that I'm a one of 'these people' – an immigrant – too. She was visibly upset and nothing I said or did calmed her down.

Part of the problem with the EU is that each European country wants to keep its particularisms while belonging to Europe. Let's take an example: in France, when a private company wants to implement a redundancy plan, it's a big deal. This means that, even if the company is not even remotely owned by the state, the government will get involved, one way or another. It's a French specificity. It's what French people expect. I'm not talking about politicians making a comment in passing and acknowledging that the local communities will have a tough ride, which is what seems to happen this side of the Channel. No, in France, the government will negotiate directly with the company in question and try, as far as possible, to prevent redundancies. Sometimes it works, sometimes it doesn't.

I wonder what will happen to French interventionism if we move towards a more federal Europe. The transition will be tough. Really tough ...

As I write, we're still in the aftermath of the 'Brexit' vote. British society is more divided than ever. Until the eve of the referendum, the 'remain' vote had an advantage in the polls, so the results of the vote took the whole world by surprise.

Some argued that it was a vote against immigration. I'm not sure. Well-educated, establishment-minded analysts – whether in journalism, finance or politics – appear to have a tendency to discount the determination of populist, conservative and less privileged voters to support candidates and policies that until now have been considered implausible, even though the polls these days indicate that these 'disenfranchised' voters could really make themselves felt. (This applied not only in the Brexit vote, but also to Trump.)

The future is a blank sheet of paper. There is one thing for sure: the debate on Britishness is here to stay, and it will be pivotal to the success of the implementation of Brexit.

Britain and the US

The UK and the US are said to have a very close relationship. So, over the last fourteen years, I've never understood why the Brits seem to hate the Americans so much. They call them Yankees or dimwits at every possible opportunity, say that they've stolen the English language and changed it, and keep criticising aspects of American policy – gun control, or lack of; extravagant use of prison sentences …

When confronted, your British friends and colleagues will insist that it's just a light-hearted dig, and that part of the problem is the fact that Americans don't do sarcasm and so on and so forth. In other words, it's their fault. Unbelievable!

Over the years I've noticed that there's a very complex cultural rivalry between Britain and America that goes way back, and I'm just far too French to understand its reasons.

I feel for my American friends who happen to be at the receiving end of such delightful comments. Because we French love the Americans, don't we? Most of the time, anyway. Let's not forget we gave them the Statue of Liberty!

The Commonwealth
Unlike we French, the British have managed to sustain good relationships with their former colonies. Don't get me wrong, it wasn't always plain sailing – but it works. So how did they do it?

I suppose they should thank us French, because from the Hundred Years' War until the defeat of Napoleon, France was their chief enemy. The baddie. Have you noticed how everything is easier when we all have a common enemy? In England's case, it was France for a very long time, and it kept everybody united (against France, in case you hadn't guessed). Can we get a medal for this, please?

To be fair, it's true that British foreign relations since 1600 had focused on achieving a balance of power, and that long-term cooperation was always a priority for Britain. In most cases, the dissolution of the British empire happened in a dignified and ceremonial manner, and led to a popularly elected government. There were lots of speeches encouraging the new nations, and most members of the Royal Family were called upon to take part in the proceedings.

The solidarity between the UK and the Commonwealth nations remains very strong, which still surprises me ... But hey, I've come to accept that I'm still learning.

CONCLUSION
SO WHAT ABOUT ME?

I need to face reality here. Despite my new British passport, I will never be considered British.

Whatever I do, wherever I go, I'm always 'the French one'. My British friends and colleagues still think of me as French. Why? Why the double standard? I have non-British colleagues from other countries who, just like me, are naturalised citizens. They're considered to be British. Sometimes someone says that they're 'Indian-born' or 'from the continent', but that's as far as it goes.

As for me, despite the fact that I've been living in London for the best part of fourteen years, I'm still, always, considered to be French.

'Ask Muriel,' someone says.

'Who's she?'

'The French one.'

But of course.

What did I do to deserve to be stigmatised like this? What do I need to do to be British? Is it my accent? Is it because I wasn't brought up in one of the posher British institutions, I wonder?

Maybe I need to learn some British poems by heart. Truth be told, I wouldn't be starting from scratch: one of my favourite poems is 'If' by Rudyard Kipling. But that's clearly not enough. I need to try harder. John Keats, Byron, Sylvia Plath maybe ... I wonder.

I also shamefully admit that, as I was educated in France, I didn't study Shakespeare. That's not entirely true: we studied a French translation of Romeo and Juliet. And yes, I think Shakespeare is overrated. Before any Brits judge me too harshly, they need to understand that I've had a crash course in Shakespeare with my children, who study at least one Shakespeare play every year. I'm starting to become an expert now. But maybe, just maybe, you need to be born over here to fully appreciate it.

And I wasn't. Enough said.

What else could it be?

Maybe it's the way I drink tea. I like a good cuppa from time to time, but that's as far as it goes. I'm more a coffee sort of girl.

Maybe it's the cricket. The fact that I don't understand the rules. My view is that cricket should be used to cure insomnia. That's just me.

Maybe it's my dress style. I don't think that I dress in a 'French' way, but who knows? You'll never see me wearing tweed or tartan. It goes against everything I stand for. As for dressing in bright yellow – I think I'll leave that to the Queen.

Maybe I need to dye my hair blonde or ginger. No way. Not in a million years. I will remain a brunette. This much I know.

Maybe I need to set up a family trust and a bank account in Panama. That would help, wouldn't it? I wish …

Ultimately, Britishness seems to be a relative concept. People see what they want to see in it. It depends on their age, their education, their family. Whatever, one thing remains certain: I do not stand a chance of being considered British.

Never have and probably never will.

I keep being asked why I'm staying in London if I feel so at odds with British ways. So here's the truth. Now that I've had my say, I must admit that I have a lot more fun over here than I ever had, or think I could have, in my home country.

Isn't that reason enough?

ABOUT THE AUTHOR

Muriel (that's Moo-ree-*elle* not *Mew*-ree-el) is a self-proclaimed French Yummy Mummy living London. She blogs at FrenchYummyMummy.com and is often featured in magazines and newspapers and asked to comment on radio and television about all things French: Muriel made the cover of *The Times* on Saturday clutching a baguette. She is an expert on all things French, and became a naturalised British citizen in 2012.

Made in the USA
Charleston, SC
16 December 2016